One Day in France

JEAN-MARIE BORZEIX is a journalist, writer and broadcaster. He began his career as a reporter writing for *Combat* and the *Quotidien de Paris* before becoming Editor-in-Chief of *Les Nouvelles Littéraires* and Literary Editor for *Éditions du Seuil*. From 1984 to 1997 he was Director of the prestigious public radio channel France Culture and later, Special Advisor to the President of the Bibliothèque Nationale de France.

GAY McAULEY is a French theatre specialist who has played a leading role in the development of performance studies in Australia. She is a distinguished research fellow in Theatre Studies at Royal Holloway College, University of London and Honorary Associate Professor in Theatre and Performance Studies, University of Sydney.

CAROLINE MOOREHEAD is the author of many books including *Village of Secrets: Defying the Nazis in Vichy France* and *A Train in Winter: A Story of Resistance, Friendship and Survival in Auschwitz*.

'A completely enthralling and disturbing account of a forgotten episode during the Nazi occupation of France in World War II. An exceptional and moving work of historical investigation.'

WILLIAM BOYD

'The distant sounds from neighbouring hamlets, the suspicions, the waiting for bad news, the secret flights along paths unknown to the military, the explosions and then silence once more, heavy, unbearable… Jean-Marie Borzeix has pulled off an extraordinary feat.'

BERNARD PIVOT

ONE DAY IN FRANCE

TRAGEDY AND BETRAYAL IN AN OCCUPIED VILLAGE

JEAN-MARIE BORZEIX

Translated by Gay McAuley

Foreword by Caroline Moorehead

[signature]

I.B. TAURIS

LONDON · NEW YORK

Published in 2016 by
I.B. Tauris & Co. Ltd
London • New York
www.ibtauris.com

Copyright © Éditions Stock, 2008, 2016 Jean-Marie Borzeix
Copyright translation and translator's note © Gay McAuley
Copyright foreword © Caroline Moorehead

ISBN: 978 1 78453 622 0
eISBN: 978 0 85772 868 5

A full CIP record for this book is available from the British Library
A full CIP record is available from the Library of Congress

Library of Congress Catalog Card Number: available

Text designed and typeset by Tetragon, London
Printed and bound in Sweden by ScandBook AB

For Noémie and Valérian

Contents

List of Illustrations

The nature of these images makes it impossible in most cases to credit the photographers. Grateful thanks to members of the victims' families, notably the Rozent family in Israel, Daniel Wagner, Renée and Myriam Schwartz, Henry Fribourg and Jean-Bernard Hoch, who have authorised the reproduction of some of their precious photographs, rare traces of the lives that were so brutally extinguished.

Photographs of Bugeat during the war and earlier were generously provided by Pierre Fournet, Yves Orliange and Jean-Yves Urbain, and Barry Thomas kindly took photographs of Bugeat today. The photograph of Malka Rozent by her husband's grave in 1945 was discovered only in 2015 by Jean-Louis Beynat when sorting his late grandfather's papers, a perfect example of the way information about the past is continually coming to light.

Occupied France, 1940–5

Bugeat and environs

Foreword

ON 8 NOVEMBER 1942, BRITISH AND AMERICAN forces landed in North Africa. Three days later, just as it grew light, the Wehrmacht, fearing an Allied landing on France's Mediterranean coast, crossed the demarcation line that had previously separated the German-held north from the Vichy south and occupied the whole country. From that moment on, no one was safe: not the Resistance, whose numbers were increasing all the time and who had found security of a kind in the previously unoccupied zone; not ordinary people suspected of anti-German and anti-Vichy sentiments; and certainly not the Jews.

From now until the Liberation of France in the summer of 1944, some nineteen months later, villages, hamlets, towns, remote country areas everywhere were subject to *rafles*, round-ups, whether of hostages to shoot in reprisal for attacks on German soldiers, or of Jews, to be deported to the death camps in Poland. *One Day in France*, like a Greek tragedy, is the account of what happened on a single day in the spring of 1944, 6 April, on one small plateau in the Corrèze in central France, when a group of

SS soldiers with their death's head insignia descended on the area. This is history viewed through a magnifying glass, using one forgotten event in one place to tell the story of what the French call *les années noires,* the dark and terrifying years of German occupation and French collaboration.

Jean-Marie Borzeix is a distinguished and successful cultural journalist and editor, and the former director of France's prestigious public radio channel, France Culture. In 2001, he found himself travelling repeatedly between Paris and the small market town of Bugeat, which lies some 200 kilometres south-west of Clermont-Ferrand, just north of Brive, in order to visit his father, who was ill. Borzeix himself is a native of the area, having been born in Bugeat in the summer of 1941. It was just near here, in the little village of L'Echameil, that the tragic events which he describes in *One Day in France* took place.

Borzeix's tale follows three separate strands, each entwined with the other, one story feeding into another, but all with a slightly different background. What started as a journalist's simple curiosity, the desire to discover more about the war in the Corrèze, spread bit by bit as he learned more, and saw how hard it was to unearth facts long left buried. His first thought was to seek out and interview the survivors and their descendants: interviewing, as he once said, was in his journalist blood. Soon, however, he found himself faced with great gaps in knowledge and memory, holes in the story that could only be plugged through deeper archival research. He turned to the excellent departmental and national libraries of which France is justly proud. But by now he had also been bitten by another bug, something very familiar to the French, a fascination with the process of memory itself, what is recalled and how, and what is lost and why, and this too he decided to weave into the narrative of his book.

By the spring of 1944, when the story at the heart of *One Day in France* begins, plans were already being finalised for the invasion and liberation of France, in which the Resistance and the maquis, hiding out in the mountainous areas of central and southern France, intended to play a major role. Across the Limousin and the Haute-Loire, for many miles all around Bugeat and L'Echameil, there were some fourteen different groups of maquisards, gathered under three overarching umbrellas: that of the Gaullist Armée Secrète, that of the Mouvements Unis de la Résistance, and that of the fighting arm of the communist Francs-Tireurs et Partisans Français. Many of these young maquisards were local boys, evading the draft of the Service du Travail Obligatoire, the STO, under which young Frenchmen were dispatched to Germany to help the war industry. They spent their nights high in the mountains, in hiding, and were provisioned by their families in the villages and hamlets below, or by men and women known as the 'legals', who pursued ordinary lives, with ordinary occupations on the surface, but who at the same time provided secret help to the underground. As the spring of 1944 advanced, so the attacks by the maquis on the Germans multiplied. Convoys were ambushed, trains derailed, depots bombed, soldiers killed.

The events that took place on that Holy Thursday in 1944 were a direct consequence of one such maquisard attack, in which a number of German officers had been ambushed. Their comrades were after revenge. Though less barbaric than the better-known reprisals that took place in the nearby town of Tulle soon after, when ninety-nine men and boys were hanged from lamp posts, trees and balconies as punishment for a successful maquis assault, the apparently random, calm, almost mechanical selection and execution of four innocent men among the inhabitants of L'Echameil has the same chilling mercilessness. In Tulle, the German troops drank and laughed while the bodies swung in the air; in L'Echameil, the Wehrmacht soldiers left behind cheerfully set about making preparations for an Easter feast. Uncovering and describing the identity of the local men chosen as victims, the negotiations preceding their execution and the execution itself, form the first strand of Borzeix's narrative.

The second concerns a Jewish violinist, father of two young daughters and about to become a father for the third time. Haïm Rozent's capture and subsequent killing belongs not to the need to punish hostages but to the Germans' round-up of the Jews. Once again, failing to find enough information through his interviews, Borzeix turned to the archives. These yielded remarkable material.

When the Germans invaded France in May 1940, and cut the country in two, they were not yet planning to make it *Judenfrei*, free of Jews, for that still lay in the future. Rather, what they had in mind was to use the zone ruled over – at least nominally – by Marshal Pétain and his Vichy government as a reception centre for all those unwanted Jews who had resided until then in the north. Those that fled south with the great exodus of May and June 1940, when some 6 million terrified people took to the roads in cars, milk floats, hearses, on bicycles and horseback, on their feet, dragging behind them cases, small children, even animals, were not to be allowed back across the demarcation line. They settled, in various degrees of safety, across the Vichy zone, some of them in and around L'Echameil and Bugeat.

By the spring of 1944, however, things had moved on. Vichy's anti-Semitism very nearly matched that of the German occupiers and Pétain and his head of government, Pierre Laval, had been quick to anticipate German wishes. Between 8 October 1940 and 16 September 1941, Vichy pushed through twenty-six laws, twenty-four decrees, six by-laws and one regulation on the Jews, effectively disenfranchising them and banning them from a wide range of professions and occupations. The 150,000 or so foreign Jews among them, who had settled in France during the more welcoming 1920s and 1930s, when foreign workers were needed to make up for the 1.5 million Frenchmen who had died in World War I, had quickly been rounded up and put into internment camps. From here, all through 1942 and 1943, they had been handed over to the Germans and deported from the station of Drancy, on the outskirts of Paris, to the extermination camp of Auschwitz. In exchange, Pétain and Laval had asked for, and briefly obtained, an agreement that, for the moment at least, French Jews would be safe.

That deal, however, had not lasted long. Once most of the foreign Jews had been taken, the Germans turned their eyes towards the French ones. The trains leaving Drancy now contained not only Polish, Russian, German, Lithuanian and Italian Jews, but French families, long assimilated into French life, many believing themselves to be essentially French, and not Jewish at all. In L'Echameil as in other hamlets and towns across the Haute-Loire and the Corrèze, the hunt was now on for all remaining Jews, whether French or foreign. That those who were French believed that they were safe made it all the easier for the Germans to track them down. Though Rozent and his family were originally Polish, having come to France only in 1940, they had lived in the area for several years and they, too, had believed themselves secure. Their French neighbours were friends; they felt themselves protected. What happened to Chaim and his family on 6 April, and to ten other local Jews, arrested on the same day, was happening every day all over France, with the same tragic consequences.

By the time France was liberated, some 75,000 Jews had been deported, the majority of them foreign. Not many more than 2,500 came home. The last train to leave Drancy for Auschwitz, with over 300 children on board, did not depart until 31 July 1944, by which time de Gaulle's forces were already advancing on Paris. That some 300,000 Jews survived the Holocaust in France – which made it one of the highest survival rates in Europe – says much about the courage and generous spiritedness of the inhabitants of places like L'Echameil and Bugeat. Though neither of those places ever acquired the renown of the Plateau Vivarais-Lignon, or Dieulefit, where local inhabitants consciously set out to save Jews, it is heartening to read about the selfless way in which many perfectly ordinary French men and women behaved. Had others behaved so imaginatively, with so little regard to their own well-being, the picture would have been better still.

One Day in France's third strand touches on another, endlessly fascinating, aspect of France and its years of occupation. It is about memory. No European country has been as interested as France in the subject of memory and history, how they are perceived, understood, recorded, arranged, rearranged and transmitted. This obsession with memory as a fluid, living, endlessly changing phenomenon, something in constant evolution, dates back to 1929, when Marc Bloch and Lucien Febvre founded the Annales school. In what have been described as the 'memory wars', French historians, 'militants of memory', have picked over the past, questioning, evaluating, reshaping its contours. There are said today to be some 100,000 *'lieux de mémoire'*, sites of remembrance, in France, and these are not only actual places, monuments and sites, but people and even ideas. While researching his book, Borzeix became engrossed by the part played by memory in his story, the way that some of his witnesses remembered some things, others quite different ones, others again, nothing at all.

France has had trouble coming to term with its *années noires*. The stain left by collaboration has if anything spread, as more and more people have been forced to acknowledge what took place. For many years – decades – encouraged by de Gaulle's determination to put the past behind and reconstruct a strong and independent France, it was easier to lay the blame on a small number of rotten apples. It was not until Marcel Ophuls's remarkable film *Le Chagrin et la Pitié*, in 1969, and Robert Paxton's *Vichy France: Old Guard and New Order*, which appeared in 1972, that France's complicity in the murder of the Jews was seriously debated, and not until the 1980s and 1990s that some of the most notorious

French collaborators – Klaus Barbie, René Bousquet, Maurice Papon – were finally brought to trial.

One result of the long delay in facing up to wartime crimes has been to obscure the events of those years, to cover them with a film of amnesia, to make them seem even more fluid and elusive; and, in some cases, to make the very mention of them toxic. During the long quest for the identity of the man who had betrayed Jean Moulin to the Gestapo, the names of two heroes of the Resistance, Lucie and Raymond Aubrac, were mentioned. They had been blameless, but for some years this now elderly couple was subject to hurtful accusations.

What Borzeix discovered among some of those he interviewed was not just forgetfulness, but what he calls a *'refoulement collectif'*, a wilful collective pushing back, rejecting, repression of the memory of those times. Seeking clarity and facts, he was driven ever deeper into the archives, where his patient sleuthing uncovered many unexpected things. His aim, he said, was not to find culprits, the names of those who may have given the Jews away, but to 'retrieve the dead from the forgetting' into which they had been cast.

In the late 1940s, the playwright and author Charlotte Delbo, who was one of the very few French survivors of Auschwitz, sat down and wrote about her experiences. Then she put her account to one side, and left it there, unlooked at, for twenty years. She wanted to be certain that her words stood the test of time, and really did convey what it had actually felt like to be in a death camp. By making her prose absolutely plain, completely transparent, with no embellishment, no adjectives, she hoped that nothing would come between the reader and his understanding. *Auschwitz and After*, published finally in the 1970s, is as immediate and haunting a portrait of the Holocaust as the works of Primo Levi.

When writing *One Day in France*, Borzeix reached the same decision. In order to give back life and dignity to the men and women whose sad stories he tells, he set out to write as simply and clearly as he could, his words '*dépouillées*', as shorn, bald, bare as he could make them, as he told a reporter. As with Delbo and Levi, the short, stark sentences, and the absence of any trace of floweriness, lend the narrative great strength.

CAROLINE MOOREHEAD
DECEMBER 2015

Preface

IN CREATING THIS ACCOUNT OF A PAST TIME, I HAVE HAD to contend with both amnesia and the temptation to embroider. Each fragment of the stories unearthed and told here helps to reconstruct the larger picture of a reality that is gone forever, but that at times seems as close as yesterday, at times as remote as an episode of the Thirty Years War.

My word will have to be trusted, for many of the witnesses are no longer with us. They have taken to their graves the minute details of a reality that only they could vouch for. Furthermore, because archival searches can never be complete – a new piece of information, discovered by mere chance, can cast an entirely new light on past events – this account of what happened in the French countryside must remain open. In the future, further details will certainly emerge, revisions will be made. Nothing would be more foolish than to claim that I have produced a definitive version of the history of that time. As it has turned out, despite my best efforts, history and memory remain inextricably entwined. Nevertheless, everything in this account is credible, and my endeavour at all times has been to uncover the truth.

The events recounted here occurred in mountainous terrain, a country of low ranges, plateaus, moorland, woods and meadows, remote from urban centres and their reliable means of communication. Towards the end of World War II, similar events occurred in France in many other provincial capitals that resemble this one. It can certainly be claimed that in many villages and small towns all over Europe, the atrocities committed and the sufferings endured were far worse, far more worthy of interest. The horror that occurred more than half a century ago in this little market town in the Limousin has no pretension to rival those in thousands of Polish, Ukrainian, Russian, Serb, Greek, Italian and German villages, all of which produced hundreds of thousands, even millions, of victims during the same war. It is different and yet similar, banal and yet unique. Suffering cannot be qualified as major or minor.

The places where these events occurred can be found on maps. The victims and their families are referred to by their real names. This retrospective investigation belongs to them as well as to the many more who are not named: the inhabitants of the canton,[1] living and dead, who shared their memories with me and to whom I express my gratitude.

L'Echameil

Haute-Corrèze, 6 April 1944

THE WEATHER IS MAGNIFICENT, THE AIR CRYSTAL clear as so often in that high country when the hoar frosts ease and the spring rains become less frequent. That morning the dawn chorus begins earlier and the birds sing more loudly. It is the time of year when gardeners hurry to rake up the last leaves and create great bonfires that they set alight with the cheerful sense that the old year is finally over and done with. On that day, many wisps of pale smoke can be seen in the distance, rising gently into the early morning sky.

But the smoke that rises suddenly from the tiny village of L'Echameil is different, darker and thicker. The inhabitants of the neighbouring hamlets do not have to look twice to know that. Those closest to the village have in any case been expecting something. When the air is so clear, sound travels with the precision of light, and villagers have always cultivated the habit of listening to the sounds coming from neighbouring villages, in spite of the trees and hedgerows that separate them, just as town dwellers eavesdrop on their next door neighbours. Shortly before nine in the morning, people in Broussouloux and Champseix had heard the loose planks on the bridge across the stream clatter more loudly than usual, a sign that the trucks making their way to L'Echameil were not local. Besides, the engines sounded lighter than the wheezing of the villagers' gas producers.

They had heard the dogs yelping. More significant was the shouting that had followed, and they had listened intently to the yells and stifled cries that were not like any ordinary quarrel, to the foreign sounding language, more guttural and abrupt than any expression of anger in the Limousin dialect. Then silence, a very long silence, then some more shouts, orders rather than argument. Then that dark plume of smoke. Then the loose planks of the bridge had clattered again. Then absolute silence. And the knowledge that something terrible has happened.

A brave man living in the closest of the neighbouring villages runs down across the steeply sloping fields. To give help, to get news. In the village, an elderly woman is wringing her hands, repeating over and over in the old dialect '*Lou jou atrapa!*', 'They have taken them!' The men have indeed gone. Left behind are the wives and mothers of three of them, silent and devastated. The Vacher family house has been set on fire, the interior is already gutted and flames are beginning to attack the roof. The doors of all the other houses and barns opening onto the village square are wide open, as though half the inhabitants had stepped out, just for a moment. The young man races home to tell, breathlessly, what he has seen. The people listening to him go pale and say nothing.

In the market town of Bugeat, the parish priest has opened the church early and is in the sacristy, getting things ready for the Holy Week services. This is the Thursday before Easter, when as well as celebrating the daily mass, he must prepare the holy water and the great Paschal candle that are to be blessed in later services. In the shops, customers are more hurried, less talkative than usual.

They are worried about their children. As it is the first day of the short Easter school holiday, some of the boys left at dawn on their bicycles to go and fetch the huge loaves of bread that, since the beginning of the war, people have been taking to be baked in the old-fashioned way in the bread ovens of farms scattered around the countryside.

Returning with their loads at nine or ten o'clock and sweating as they pedal hard up the hills, the boys suddenly jam on their brakes and stop short when they see in the distance – from the turning before the bridge to Rochers, from the edge of the woods at Chaleix, from the last bend before Vezou – that soldiers have taken up positions at different entrances to the town. Although they have not had much contact with the German army, who rarely enter this part of the country that is of little strategic importance to them, the boys know immediately that the figures they can see in the distance are German soldiers. They observe that soldiers are posted at regular intervals on all the roads. The town is surrounded.

But these boys are on their home ground, they know every footpath and track and they slip easily through the net. They are afraid, excited; this time, at last, it is really war. Suddenly, they are no longer children. But at the same time it is still a game.

A dozen military vehicles are occupying one of the town squares while an armoured car with a machine gun mounted on the back is patrolling the surrounding streets. On the back of all these vehicles a large letter 'B' has been painted in white.

Soldiers have taken over the boys' school which adjoins the *mairie*, as is the long-standing custom in republican France. They have rolled their camp kitchen to the centre of the schoolyard, and in the covered playground they have tethered a magnificent cow, 'requisitioned' along the way. The rumour spreads that the cow was found in a stable as they came through Limoges. Did one of the soldiers let slip this piece of information? For months now, people have developed the habit of speaking very little and of passing on in whispers any detail of information gleaned from neighbours. But how can one distinguish true from false when it is so difficult to travel, when the newspapers are themselves full of lies and omissions? Needless to say, for several days now, the telephone lines have been cut in this part of the region.

Each canton is unaware of what is happening in the neighbouring canton, each commune is cut off from the surrounding communes. Nevertheless, people are continually aware of the violence that hovers in their midst. Word spreads that yesterday, in Lacelle, several men were killed. In Lonzac too. The mayor, who had lost an arm in the first war, and the town clerk are said to have been shot dead somewhere near Treignac. How can people separate fact from rumour? It is known that detachments of the Wehrmacht have begun to occupy some small towns. But this does not mean that the rural areas are going to be spared. Several farms in the village of La Forêt have been torched, cattle have been slaughtered; except, of course, the magnificent cow presiding over the school playground, between the church and the *mairie*.

Towards ten o'clock a truck coming from L'Echameil drives up and parks on the central square. A truck with an uncovered platform and slatted sides, crammed with civilians and soldiers. The soldiers jump down first, then come the others, the hostages. Four peasants in heavy twill trousers who have been permitted to put on their coats, four peasants dressed to go to town, four familiar figures: Antoine Nauche, Léon Vacher, Antoine Gourinal, Léon Ganne. One of them walks with difficulty, having lost a leg as a result of his time in the trenches in the 1914 war. They are all more than forty years old; one of them is certainly nearer sixty. The soldiers hustle them roughly, as is expected, and push to one side the woman who has been brought with them. People in the houses, hiding behind their curtains, recognise Mme Vacher, wife of the injured veteran, a grey scarf tied around her head. The soldiers push the men along, as though excess brutality were no longer necessary.

Events, it seems, are taking their natural course. The president of the Special Delegation, appointed by the Vichy authorities to replace the mayor, is the last to get out of the truck into which the soldiers had thrown him so unceremoniously nearly two hours earlier. Very pale and dishevelled, embarrassed by his bedroom slippers, open shirt and absence of neck tie, he tries nevertheless to maintain the dignity of his modest municipal office. He regrets that he does not look to them like the lawyer he really is when dressed in his formal weekday clothes, his starched collar, dark suit and well-polished shoes. Who knows, this might have had some influence on the German officer, might have stirred a vestige of class complicity. But what can a provincial lawyer do when faced with the commanding officer of a troop of occupying forces hounded by 'terrorists'? Especially if this officer is a tough looking young lieutenant who, like all the other members of his squad, has a death's head embroidered onto the sleeves of his tunic.

When the soldiers had come to fetch him a little after eight o'clock that morning, he had just got up and was looking out of his window to check the new shoots beginning to show in his garden. He responded calmly to their questions and told them at the outset that there were no recalcitrants, terrorists or foreigners without proper authorisation within his jurisdiction. They had lists of names that they showed him. He scanned the lists, pretending to find nothing of interest but in fact recognising many familiar names. To the officer he said that all those listed were either not known to him, or were absent, gone far away, or unable to be contacted, lost. And after all, this was not completely untrue.

Underground fighters do not normally set up camp in the middle of town. Many young men of the region joined the Resistance in order to avoid the STO[1] and have been pursued by

the French police as draft dodgers. With the reverses suffered by
the German army in Russia, however, and with the Allied invasion of France said to be imminent, enthusiasm for this work on
the part of the local police is increasingly tempered by a degree
of caution. For nearly a year, large numbers of young men have
been joining the maquis and hiding out in remote country areas,
in the depths of the pine forests, emerging only at night. As for
the foreign families, most of them Jewish or Spanish, they are to
be found everywhere, mixing with the general population, but
they probably took to their heels as soon as they heard the first
German truck arriving.

But why had the German command decided so suddenly to
send a detachment out to L'Echameil when there were many other
villages closer to them? Why this particular village, situated far
from the main road, and consisting only of a few farmhouses
grouped around a simple square covered with thin grass, cowpats,
manure and mud? Why the special interest shown in the Vacher
family? As the officers have lists of names, and everyone here
knows that the young men of L'Echameil are in the maquis, it
seems more than likely that the German action had been planned
in advance, that it was the result of a deliberate decision, almost
certainly in response to a tip-off.

In L'Echameil, the lawyer sees it all. He defends the case of
the four men, pointing out that they were too old to fight, and
could not possibly be in the maquis. They were certainly not of
the same social strata, he a local worthy of moderate political
opinions, while they are peasant farmers, owning their own small
properties and supporting the Communist Party as do so many
others in the canton, but who cares? In an instant such differences
have become insignificant, ridiculous. He has done everything
possible to curb the anger of the German soldiers, exacerbated by
the pride of these men of the land, born and bred in this country
of rebels, men who have never bowed their heads, particularly

those who spent years fighting in the trenches. Stubborn peasants, they argue with the soldiers, try to outwit them, stand up to them, even to bluster. They never asked for mercy. When did they realise that their lives were at stake? As the official representative of the municipal authority appointed by Vichy, the lawyer tries to find arguments to persuade the lieutenant that the Resistance poster stuck on the cattle trough right at the centre of the hamlet does not mean that all the inhabitants are themselves members of the Resistance. He might have added that posters just like that one, in fact a leaflet urging the population to cease supplying food to the occupying forces, were to be found all over the countryside, that the first leaflets had been scattered during the night of 11 November 1942, that others had been tossed on several occasions into the garden of one of the leading local members of the militantly pro-Vichy Legion, the organisation set up by the government to bring together all the existing veterans' associations. He could also have added that there had been one pasted on the door of his own *mairie* the other day, and that it meant only that Resistance fighters had been in the town that night, that they were there on the ground, and that they would be back the next night, that this was their home. He would have done better to hold his tongue. The evidence of their eyes carries more weight than the cleverest arguments. In any case, the lieutenant knows that even if these peasants are not in the maquis, their sons are of the same ilk as the terrorists who a few nights before and not far from here had set an ambush in which a whole carload of German officers had been killed. Was he not there precisely to carry out a punitive action against the maquis in general and the local population who protected them? The discovery of the leaflet pasted on the cattle trough merely convinced him that all the adult males present that morning are equally responsible, equally guilty.

The lawyer hears him angrily order the four hostages to get dressed, to put on shoes and overcoats. He hears him then order his men to set fire to one of the houses in the hamlet, before taking everyone except for the oldest women. 'Enemies yesterday, enemies today, enemies forever!' The lieutenant is sure to have heard that catchcry. A few words in a language one hardly knows are all that is needed to convey the essentials. And the essential had been said before they even left the village. The hostages refuse to speak, to indicate the hideouts of the Resistance fighters they are protecting. They will never speak in any case, for it is their own sons they would be betraying. So they will be shot.

Everyone knows that this tragedy is going to play out to its appointed end. From this point onwards, everything proceeds along lines that are, if not exactly familiar, at least businesslike. There is a discussion between the officer and the town clerk who, coming from Lorraine like many of the refugees, speaks fluent German. The officer tells the clerk that he wants the hostages to be executed by firing squad here, in the middle of the town, on the square in front of the *mairie* and the church. Is this the reason people living on the square have been ordered to close their shutters? So that the execution of the hostages will not be transformed into spectacle, for fear of the reactions it might provoke among the inhabitants? To avoid creating martyrs to haunt the future? In the town, everyone finds they are speaking in hushed voices.

The lawyer protests even before the clerk has translated what is being said. The discussion continues, laborious and solemn but ultimately futile, for it is no longer about saving lives, only about saving appearances. It continues for a while until the officer gives in: the hostages will be shot outside the town. That will be the only victory for the French today. It is purely procedural, concerning the protocols of death.

The soldiers make the hostages climb back into the truck. It looks as though they are taking the road to L'Echameil, as though they are simply being driven back home again. But just outside the town, immediately after the railway bridge, the truck keeps going, along the road that leads to the cemetery. The long wall that encloses the cemetery would indeed make an ideal site to line up the hostages facing the firing squad. Isn't it well known that the Germans have a taste for such orderliness? This time, however, they prefer to go further away. They have agreed to keep well away from the town, and they will keep their word. So they stop about a kilometre beyond the river, at a path leading to a little birch wood.

On one side, the soldiers and the lieutenant. On the other, four men who are going to die. Proud men with wild eyes.

The bursts of machine gun fire can be heard for miles. The sounds stand out even more because gunshots, formerly so frequent during the hunting season, are now rarely heard since all rifles have long been requisitioned and hunting banned. In any case huntsmen make no mistake about these sounds. These shots are nothing like the discharge of buckshot used in hunting rabbit or wild boar or deer. Nor do they have anything in common with the isolated, high pitched bursts of gunfire occasionally heard from the maquis at night, when Resistance marksmen are practising or feeling bored. This time it is a concentrated group volley, heavy and sombre, followed by silence.

It will soon be midday. In the little town, the streets are deserted. News of the hostages' death is not confirmed. They were brought here and then they were taken away again. Children are called home. As lunchtime approaches, the doors close quickly. It is easy to imagine families around the table, struggling to find words to talk about the events. Under the stress of the moment, almost as a means of self-preservation, many revert to speaking the old dialect. People are in a state of shock as much as grief. Who would ever have thought that things would come to this? Hints of the German reprisals exacted in the region in recent days have hardly reached this place. Very few people have the means or the courage to venture outside the limits of the canton. The two daily newspapers, the *Courrier du Centre* and the *Appel du Centre*, have long avoided making any allusion at all to clashes between the local Resistance and the police, the militia or German soldiers. The daily column headed 'Criminality and its Repression' does in fact report incidents, ambushes and arrests, but only if they have happened on the other side of France, in the Isère, in Brittany or in the north of the country. Never in this region where, if one believed these newspapers, there is absolutely nothing happening that is worth reporting. People have learned to interpret this absence of news. They are not stupid and they cannot avoid knowing that things are getting very difficult for the occupying army. But how can one find out what is really happening only a few miles away? For the last few weeks, the whole of the department of Corrèze as well as the adjoining divisions of the neighbouring department of Haute-Vienne have been declared 'no-go zones'. A safe conduct pass is required for people who have to leave the neighbourhood, and curfew has been brought forward to six o'clock in the evening. People lucky enough to possess a radio listen to BBC broadcasts after dark, struggling to hear the words through the crackle of static interference introduced by the Germans, but these broadcasts hardly ever report on events in the immediate vicinity. Since the beginning of the war, nearly four years ago, people have become accustomed to avoiding its horrors. Many young men have joined the Resistance but, as has already been said, this is as much to escape obligatory labour in Germany as to take the fight to a faraway and often invisible enemy. But now, suddenly, the war has come here in flesh and blood. A war that is unlike that other war in 1914, a war without a front line, a war where civilians must confront the enemy.

At the beginning of the afternoon, the day seems to be trying to become a day like any other. Shops open for business but customers are few and far between. People glance quickly at each other before turning away. When the time for the Holy Thursday mass approaches, a few women make their way towards the church wearing black shawls over their heads, weaving between the military vehicles with their white painted 'B' markings. The church is next door to the school that has been taken over by the German soldiers; it is so close, in fact, that on many occasions mourners at funeral services have been disturbed by the laughter of the children playing in the school playground. The priest is finding it difficult to concentrate. He is separated from the shouting and noise of the soldiers only by the two stained glass windows overlooking the schoolyard. As he moves to and fro between altar and sacristy, the thought comes to him that some of the soldiers may wish to attend mass on Sunday. If they are still here, some of them will certainly wish to kneel before him to receive the host and his blessing on this Easter day. Among them, perhaps, the men who fired the shots, the men who murdered the four peasant farmers of L'Echameil.

In the meantime, despite the smallness of the congregation inside the church, their psalms and hymns can be heard on the other side of the school playground. At the end of the service, the priest stands in front of the altar and, following the liturgical tradition for Holy Thursday, makes the sign of the cross over the loaves of bread that are held up by members of the congregation as they file past him. When the group of black-clad women leave the church, carrying their loaves of bread, some German soldiers approach them, then fall back. Apparently abashed. Perhaps saying to themselves that these devout women could hardly be Jews or communists...

The magnificent Limousin cow, whose curvaceous flanks had been admired by the connoisseurs in the little town, ends up as expected. Rapidly slaughtered, her carcase has been cut up and taken to the butchers' shops to be prepared for cooking. Ovens in the local bakeries have also been commandeered. The soldiers, too, wish to celebrate Easter. Especially this year, far from their families and many of them recently returned from the Eastern Front, all of them are well aware of the gathering clouds. At this time of great danger and acute shortages, they are clearly intending to gorge themselves.

The silence is now absolute. The bodies of the men from L'Echameil are lying beside the road to Gourdon, and no one has yet seen them apart from a police patrol, which remained at a discreet distance, and a few passing motorists. Some people are beginning to suspect they are dead even though they do not yet know this for sure. No more unnecessary chatter, no more gossip. Inside the houses, people speak in hushed tones as though the sound of the human voice was itself unseemly, while outside the hustle and bustle of the German preparations for their feast gets louder and louder with the arrival of more vehicles and baggage wagons. Side by side, silence and noise. The prostration of grief and shameless arrogance. The non-commissioned officers supervise every detail of the preparation of their dishes by the butchers and bakers. The bright spring day reminds them of the Easter festivities of their childhood. They say that they will still be there on Sunday.

The whole town is deeply afraid. Every household is involved in some way. Those who maintain contact with the maquis are more afraid than the others. In the shops that face the high street, anxious looks accompany the silence. Who knows if a German officer is not going to appear suddenly with a list of names in his hand? No one in the town is ignorant of the fact that many of their fellow inhabitants were militant and active communists until the party was banned at the outbreak of the war. Everyone knows, opponents and sympathisers alike, that these people did not give up their beliefs and that many of them, freed by the collapse of the

German–Soviet pact, have got children in the maquis, and they provide them with food and supplies and pass information to them. Have some neighbours, more or less fervent supporters of Marshal Pétain, been tempted after all this time to tell the Germans what they know? The silence is due both to the ever-present fear and to the memory of the terrible event of that morning: by arresting the men from L'Echameil, the German army has brought the war right into the heart of every house in the town.

The tensions lessen slightly, however, in the middle of the afternoon when the lieutenant leaves the town with a little detachment of twenty or so tough looking young soldiers with forbidding, tense faces. Each man in this squad wears the death's head embroidered onto his uniform. Once the SS have gone,[2] it is only soldiers from the regular German army who are left behind to prepare the Easter festivities. Those remaining want to be good-humoured.

Many of the peasants in the canton decide to spend the night outdoors, as though they fear the aftershocks of an earthquake. After milking the cows, the inhabitants of the hamlets nearest to L'Echameil climb the hills near the ancient beech tree that, according to local belief, has been there since the time of the Crusades, and hide in the woods that overlook the surrounding countryside. The older men are fatalistic and, above all, concerned to protect their cattle. So they remain on guard in their farms, watching and waiting as they did for so many years in the trenches in Picardy and Champagne.

As for the murdered men, they spend the first night of their death lying in the wet grass, under the silent stars. As soon as he was able to get permission, late in the afternoon of Friday, the lawyer returns to L'Echameil to inform the wives that they are now widows. But an order has been issued forbidding anyone to go near the bodies of the dead men until further notice. Burial is forbidden. What is not forbidden, however, is walking along the road near where they lie. They were killed in order to provide an example, to strike fear into the hearts of the population. The deplorable spectacle of their death is simultaneously offered and withheld from the people.

There are very few cars. But a truck fitted with a gas producer traverses the town, carrying young men employed at the construction site of the dam across the river Vézère. Work on the dam was started at the beginning of the war and is now almost finished. The fine weather has put them all in a good humour but they stop their joking and laughing as their truck passes the German army billets that they pretend not to see. Going under the railway bridge, their truck takes the road to Vezou. On the other side of the river, the driver slows down as they draw near to the birch wood. The young men have only to turn their heads and they can see the dark shapes lying among the dead leaves and bushes. What they notice most, however, are the polished Sunday shoes glistening in the dew. The truck does not stop, and even tries to speed up.

In an office located just above the excitement and noise of the German army billets, the town clerk completes the death certificates for the four victims in his neat, firm handwriting. Their bodies can at last be acknowledged. The families receive permission to bury their dead the next day. No public display, no funeral procession through the streets of the town; they will be buried like pariahs.

Now that the SS unit has left, the German army detachment has settled itself comfortably in the boys' school, emptied of its pupils for the Easter holidays, and seems more concerned to rest than to hunt down Resistance fighters in the maquis. The people of the town soon get used to the presence of the German troops, who show no particular animosity towards them. A number of the Germans have recently returned from the Eastern Front and they are exhausted by the war. The detachment is part of the Brehmer Division (hence the letter 'B' painted on the trucks) and their commanding officer is a native of Trier. He speaks French and is happy to chat.

The group of young men who have just returned from working at the construction site have no intention of abandoning their plans in spite of the drama and the prevailing atmosphere of fear and anxiety. Most of them divide their time between the construction site and the maquis and several are intending to go to the clandestine dance that has been planned over many weeks and is scheduled for that Saturday evening at Toy-Viam. They are looking forward to meeting up with their pals from the maquis and with girls from neighbouring farms who will be trying to slip away from the protective control of their parents. These clandestine dances are virtually the only entertainment still to be found in the countryside. They are held in barns and their popularity among the young is enhanced by the fact that they are more or less forbidden: forbidden by the police and regarded with disapproval by the leaders of the Resistance in the maquis.

The girls and young men, coming home late, run the serious risk of being caught by German sentries in the middle of the night. The officers have requisitioned several rooms in the Hôtel de Paris, a well-respected family run business. A sentry has been posted at the entrance to the hotel and is pacing up and down while a number of drunken soldiers are celebrating noisily inside. As they slip quietly through the narrow alleys and side streets, the young men of the town witness from a distance the scene when a furious officer puts a stop to the partying. The captain has in effect come swiftly to the aid of the hotel manager who was being harassed by some of the soldiers. None of the listeners understand a word of what is being said, but the tone permits no rejoinders and has an immediate effect. Are the German soldiers being told off? The young men are delighted and take advantage of the upset to slip quietly into their houses without waking their parents.

During the day, it is increasingly difficult to keep the children cooped up indoors. As soon as they go out into the square, however, even though told not to, they approach the German soldiers, attracted by the noise and commotion, the uniforms and weapons, the strange way the soldiers speak, their brash self-confidence. They laugh to see the soldiers throwing scraps to the hens that wander around the square, hoping probably to obtain a few eggs from the owners. The little girls are more curious than the boys, especially the bolder ones. The soldiers, charmed and amused, are soon offering little trinkets, letting the children play with their equipment. They communicate with their hands. They roar with laughter when a cheeky little girl puts one of their helmets over her mop of curls, her whole head disappearing inside so that only her chin is showing. From behind the curtains around the square, the scene is observed by many eyes. But not one of the invisible, silent observers is tempted for a moment to laugh. The little girl is the daughter of one of the local Resistance leaders, one of the men who every night maintain contact with the clandestine fighters hiding in the maquis.

Easter Day will not be a feast day this year in spite of the smell of good food coming from the German army encampment. A thick fog will rise from the river at dawn and will gradually blot out the plain of Arvis, and then slowly envelop the cemetery where the four graves have just been closed.

The solders will leave the town in the middle of the following week.

As the teachers are quickly tidying up their classrooms, someone finds an empty *Feldpost* envelope lying around. A letter was to have been sent to Frau Lisbeth Kremer, someone's wife or girlfriend, but it was never written. The town clerk picks up the envelope and carefully puts in his desk the little rectangle of paper covered with gothic script, the only material trace that remains of the invaders' presence. The teachers apply for assistance to clean up the school premises, for the horror that has engulfed the country cannot be permitted to disrupt the school year. On the blackboard they write with exemplary care the date of the first day of class, paying attention to the downstrokes and upstrokes of their running script. The Easter holidays are over.

Living Testimony

Haute-Corrèze, Autumn 2001

I HAVE RECONSTRUCTED THE EVENTS AS THEY UNFOLDED on Holy Thursday 1944 and the days following by talking to elderly inhabitants of the market town of Bugeat and nearby villages and piecing together their accounts. They all remember their own version, nearly always with a detail which for that person illustrates and sums up the whole event, like a photographic close-up that focuses attention and obscures the surrounding landscape. Together they confirm the broad outline of this shared history. But I suspect, and am continually finding evidence, that the story is incomplete and uncertain, and will remain so because the last survivors are dying and omitting to tell all they know. Several have indeed passed away since I recorded their memories. Others who agreed to meet me have died before I could come back and talk to them. The story emerges from a huge amount of first hand testimony that was neither freely offered nor withheld.

*

Hoping to collect some final details about the events that occurred here more than half a century ago, I thought it preferable to time my visit for the end of the year. So I waited for the wet weather, the hoar frosts and mist, the daylight that begins to fade in the middle of the afternoon, the damp chill that brings people together around the fireplace or kitchen stove in the few houses that have not yet installed central heating. It might be thought that climate has no bearing on the question. But it seems to me that memories come more easily when night is falling and people are at home among friends. Is this an illusion, a superstition? On some evenings the silence is so complete that a dead leaf, frozen stiff by the first frosts and blowing through the empty streets of the town, makes a noise that seems to fill the whole space. As if there are no longer any inhabitants alive, as if the past has finally triumphed over the present and vanquished it once and for all.

After All Saints' Day, the owners of holiday homes disappear along with the last mushroom gatherers. The countryside finds itself once again with its five inhabitants per square kilometre, sometimes even fewer. In other places in the world, in the sub-Saharan area of the Aurès, or in the Sinai desert, for example, in places that are much poorer than this one, there are always groups of children who seem to emerge from nowhere and crowd around any adults present. Here, there are hardly any children any more. In the whole canton, churches open their doors more frequently for funerals than for weddings. Businesses that have been here for generations are, in recent years, like the human inhabitants, dying of exhaustion. Customers get used to patronising the nearby large supermarkets until, one morning, the village shop lacks the strength even to open its iron shutters.

People are not, however, simply resigning themselves to the inevitable demographic and economic decline. Local groups and associations are making great efforts to launch new projects, and the few young people who are choosing to come and live on the

Plateau de Millevaches see encouraging signs of new growth in
the area. Everyone is holding their breath, awaiting the results
of the most recent census. It seems, indeed, that the process of
depopulation that began almost a century ago has perhaps come
to an end and that the statisticians' graphs are about to show a
reversal of the downward trend.

During the war things were very different, and this part of the
country was full of a very cosmopolitan mix of young people. The
local population was swollen by the sudden arrival of refugees
from Paris, Lorraine, Belgium and other places, part of the mass
exodus, and they were joined by many others who arrived almost
by chance, having managed to cross the demarcation line between
occupied and Vichy controlled France, and others drawn by the
possibility of work offered by the construction of the dam on the
river Vézère. All the houses were open, all the rooms were occupied, even barns and attics. Half a century later, after a summer
season that has again failed to deliver the hoped-for miracle, it is
the past that comes to the fore with renewed vitality in the autumn.

The people I have been interviewing are for the most part over
eighty years old. The events I am questioning them about are,
as they say, 'etched' in their minds. Whether they are taciturn or
voluble, however, most of them claim at the outset that they have
forgotten everything. They begin by saying, 'Oh, you know, it's
a long time ago,' raising their eyes to the heavens. Then after an
hour or so of conversation, to hold onto a vivid moment that
seems to float like an iceberg in the midst of their failing memory,
they will admit 'for me, it's as if it happened yesterday...' But, of
course, it was not yesterday.

I ask my interviewees to dig deep in their memories, to go down
into a well that, while it may not have completely dried up, has
usually not produced any water for many years. While I descend
with them into the past, we also talk about the progress that is

being made with renovations to the retirement home. This is being enlarged again, and this time they are building accommodation specially designed for the increasing number of old people afflicted with Alzheimer's disease. The illness for which there is no cure. Every day, whole blocks of memory are shredded and dissolved. I am involved in a race against one of the worst afflictions of our age, the destroyer of memory, and it is spreading like an epidemic.

Memory loss is not, however, my only problem. I must be continually aware of the unreliability of accounts dredged up from beneath half a century of daily life. A little while ago, in Paris, I heard a lecture on the history of the Resistance by Daniel Cordier, former secretary to Jean Moulin, in which he explained why he, a highly successful art dealer, had decided at a certain time in his life to change professions and become a historian. With the caustic wit typical of the underground fighters, he recounted numerous examples of the times he had been shocked to hear apparently respectable people solemnly imparting information about the underground, the maquis and all the rest that was erroneous, completely wrong or absolute rubbish. If people generally remember material facts about the event they are recounting in extraordinary, even obsessive, detail (it was raining, night was just falling, an old lady was crossing the street, the swallows were nesting, the lamp bulb had just blown, and so on), they are often incapable of locating the event accurately in time. Was it the same day or the next; was it the same month or the next; was it even the same year? Besides this, witnesses have a natural propensity to retain, 'etched' in their memories, things that happened to them, but to have a much vaguer memory of events involving their near neighbours. Frequently misled, Daniel Cordier says he now trusts only written documents and the rare oral testimony that can be confirmed by other sources. The amateur historian has become the doubting Thomas of contemporary history.

*

This is not my case, even though I agree that local history deserves at least as much respect as the mainstream history discussed in school textbooks, on television and in the newspapers. I thought at the beginning that there would be relatively few written documents concerning the events that interested me in Bugeat. I always knew that I would have to go to consult the departmental archives and that I would need to follow up reports held by French police forces and the German regiments. All the time I was interviewing people, I was saying to myself that later on I would compare their oral testimony with the written record, that this would be the final stage of the work, the proof of accuracy. But here too, it is going to be a matter of chance, and I am aware that the archives available to me contain only those documents that have survived the negligence, the panic, the incendiary bombs, the self interested precautions, deliberate destruction and accidental loss. I comfort myself by saying that this is in any case not an official history, but simply an attempt to throw some light on one small event, a tiny detail in the overall story of the war, an event like others that occur in all wars, and are doubtless still occurring, in Iraq, in Chechnya, in Darfur, in Afghanistan, in Colombia. A remote corner of the war that is of interest to nobody except those who can think of nothing else until the day they die.

I knock on doors where I have never knocked before. I am welcomed and invited to come in and sit down, because I was born in this town, because my whole family comes from the region, because my family tree is deeply rooted in this place, because I am the son of Jeanne, the grandson of Rachel, the nephew of René, all of whom are now deceased; René more than half a century ago, Rachel over thirty years, Jeanne more than ten years ago. They may be dead but they all occupy a precise place in each person's memory. I can tell that people are wondering why I have developed such an interest in that period, that period in particular in their shared history. There were no famous Resistance fighters, no collaborators, no heroes or victims in my family. Mobilised a month after his marriage, decorated for an act of bravery on the front line in Alsace during the phoney war, returning uninjured after traversing France on foot, mostly at night and under cover, my father shared the enormous relief of the majority of the population when he heard the victor of Verdun make the country 'a gift of his person'. A staunch supporter of Pétain at the beginning of the Occupation, he joined the Resistance in the last months of the war, preparing the ground for allied parachute landings in the north of France, near Montereau (Seine-et-Marne) where he was working at the time. At the Liberation he naturally became a supporter of de Gaulle and remained so throughout the rest of his life. This very ordinary background explains nothing. Regrettable it may be, but my political genealogy provides no clue as to why I am asking these questions.

I sense that the curiosity of my interviewees is all the more acute for being unspoken. Why on earth does he want to talk about these things that it pains us to remember, why is he so determined to bring up all these stories of tragedy, of survival, of courage and cowardice, why not let us forget once and for all the cruel sequence of events that led to the death of four men in the village of L'Echameil? Why stir up the memory of the Spanish Republicans, who cut peat and lived in work camps and on neighbouring farms, or of the Jewish families scattered through the region, or indeed of the gypsy tribe who spent the war under arrest, confined to the outskirts of the town? So many people who spent a short time 'here with us', but who left more than half a century ago and, for the most part, have never been heard from again. Why does he want to disturb all these ghosts?

Nobody here would dream of making any kind of link with my grandmother's name and I am convinced that she herself never knew why her given name was a Jewish one. Why, indeed, was she given such an unusual first name in the pious Roman Catholic peasant family into which she was born in 1890, a family in which no one would have presumed to read the Bible? I have discovered, however, that there was another Rachel in the same generation, of peasant origin like her, who is listed among her close relatives. Was there perhaps a fashion for Jewish names in some peasant communities in the dying years of the nineteenth century, a faint echo of Renan's *Life of Jesus* or in response to the Dreyfus affair? I am not convinced by this explanation, which seems highly improbable. It is more likely to have been the influence of one of those missionaries who used to travel around the countryside, erecting crucifixes outside villages and preaching a return to the Bible.

Jews were referred to in church on Sunday, when the priest read the Epistles and the Gospel, but most people would have been at a loss to describe precisely who they were. Their knowledge of Jews extended only to a few clichés: they once lived in an exotic land full of palm trees, they often wore beards and loose cotton robes like Arabs, they spoke Hebrew. Practising Christians were of course aware that Jews were contemporaries of Jesus and that they were very religious, but they had great difficulty in accepting that Mary, Joseph and even Jesus himself were Jews, though this was irrefutable if only you thought about it a little. In spite of the lessons they had learned with their catechism, most remained sceptical and it would not enter their mind to acknowledge that the Christ on the crucifixes was a Jew, that it was a Jew who bore the inscription *Ecce Homo* or *I.N.R.I.* and was bedecked with fronds of boxwood on Palm Sunday.

Nobody in country areas of France, apart from those who had driven hackney cabs, or later taxis, in Paris, had ever met a Jew until certain families began to arrive at the beginning of the summer of 1940. In all the chaos of the exodus, these families were pointed out, mysteriously, by other town folk who arrived at the same time and seemed to know all about that kind of thing. People in this part of France were long-standing supporters of the republic and passionate secularists, and they had moved from radicalism to socialism in the space of only twenty years at the beginning of the century, before enthusiastically turning to the Communist Party in the weeks following the Congress of Tours. They had never shown the least interest in racism or anti-Semitism and there was probably not one man in the whole canton who would have felt the visceral hatred of a man like Maurras,[1] writing in August 1940 to his mistress, Mme Debrand, in words he spits out like weapons: 'That race is clearly the cause of it all, civil war and war between countries. They will pay the price and so they should.' In this part of the country, the atavistic anti-Semitism of the far right had no currency. It found no ground in which to grow.

My grandmother, with her curious Jewish given name, was thus known above all for being part of a traditional and pro-foundly Catholic peasant family (her sister Eugénie had entered a convent, and her nephew Fernand was a priest in the diocese), for having lost her husband in the mud of the beetroot fields of the Pas-de-Calais during the repeated offensives of 1915, for having with great difficulty and great merit brought up her two children, 'orphans of the nation', in a decent manner, and for the mourning that she put on when she was twenty-five years old and wore for the rest of her life. The fact that she had died many years previously is not important: it is her grandson who is being welcomed, and he is not an outsider here. If I am flattered to be recognised and accepted as a member of the community in this way, I am also aware that it is only a partial advantage. In spite of the hesitations and ambiguous hints that I encourage, I have been in effect catalogued from the outset, affiliated to one camp, my reactions anticipated, predicted and predictable. Something that I resist strenuously.

The question must arise often, I suppose, in the minds of my interviewees: why am I engaged in an inquiry that, on the face of it, has so little to do with me? Even I do not really know the answer. I sense only that what I am searching for in this modest inquiry, where I am groping in the dark, is an answer to questions that have haunted me since my childhood. How can one not be haunted at some time by what the poet Jules Supervielle called our 'forgetful memory'?

Nothing is explicit or definitive in relation to the last war, about which insinuations speak louder than confessions. It is partly because the two main branches of the armed Resistance – the FTP (largely dominated by the communists) and the AS (which accounted for most of the others, linked rather with the Free French)* – were in fierce competition with each other, and partly because the clandestine nature of the struggle implicated the whole population in one way or another, that the old suspicions are still far from being dispelled. Everyone knows what the other knows, or rather everyone guesses what the other one thinks he knows. No one speaks about the things that preoccupy them most, the hidden history, partly true and partly imagined, of denunciations, executions, betrayals and profiteering from goods supplied in Allied parachute drops. For some obscure reason, popular memory in relation to tragic episodes always emphasises the darker side of the story. The silences, rumours, suspicions, jealousies and insinuations I remember from my childhood are what push me now, half a century later, to enquire into the events of winter 1943 and spring 1944, when the Resistance emerged from the shadows to organise armed struggle, and when the war, with a real army and real insurgents, previously under cover, burst out and took the country by surprise.

That Holy Thursday, when the men from L'Echameil were murdered, was the war in action. A story that has become a page

---

* FTP – Francs-Tireurs et Partisans [Free Shooters and Partisans] and AS – L'Armée Secrète [The Secret Army].

in History. It is a story, too, that in the telling respects the basic rules of classical tragedy. The sudden intervention of Fate interrupting the daily course of events, the heroic response demanded, the admirable sacrifice of those who died to save their children.

I had heard this simple, powerful story told many times in the years following the Liberation and I think I have succeeded in putting together all the details here. It is dramatic, edifying, irrefutable. In a word, legendary.

Flashback

Poland, Belgium, France, Israel, 1910–2001

W HILE I AM COLLECTING SOME ADDITIONAL TESTI-
monies concerning the sequence of events on 6 April
1944, the *mairie* in Bugeat receives a letter.

A disturbing letter, sent by the French Committee for Yad
Vashem. This association, under the patronage of Samuel Pisar,
Simone Veil and Elie Wiesel, was set up to educate people in
France about the Shoah, to ensure that it is remembered, and to
recognise 'the Righteous among the Nations'. Inspired by the
belief that 'he who saves a life saves the whole world', it has been
working doggedly over the past fifty years to identify all those
people who protected Jews and saved them from deportation
and death during the last war. As I now find out, it also keeps a
watchful eye on the maintenance of the graves of Jewish victims
of the Nazis, as indicated by its Hebrew name: 'And to them
will I give in my house and within my walls a memorial (*yad*)
and a name (*shem*) that shall not be cut off.' Isaiah, chapter 56,
verse 5. It is not surprising to find Elie Wiesel associated with an

undertaking of this sort of Jewish memorialising. His whole life has been haunted by the horror that is so difficult even to name. I used to meet him on his frequent visits to Paris, and we talked about banal and trivial things, about the literary scene in Paris, about our children, our travels, the advice he was giving at the time to the president of the United States, to François Mitterrand, because he was fascinated at the time by the newly elected French president whom he had just met... I knew, however, that any such conversation was merely a temporary diversion for him. His obsession with what, under the influence of Claude Lanzmann, we were beginning to call the Shoah, weighed on him with the force of a divine commandment. He knew at first hand what he was talking about. He was deported when he was fifteen years old, and the first thing he saw on arrival at Auschwitz was a truck tipping into an open pit, as though it were simply rubble, a full load of children's bodies. He saw the small corpses on fire. 'Yes, I saw it, with my own eyes. The bodies of children burning. (Is it surprising then that since that time I have not been able to close my eyes in sleep?)' he wrote in *Night*, his first book, published in 1958 by Éditions de Minuit. He is one of the people who have taught me the elementary facts about these deeds that are so monstrous, so unthinkable that we, non-Jewish French people, for a long time simply averted our gaze. It was he, I believe, who taught me the distinction between concentration camp and death camp, and who made me begin to confront what Jews had suffered at the hands of the Nazis and their allies.

The letter from Yad Vashem draws the mayor's attention to a certain Haïm Rozent, 'arrested with a number of other members of his Resistance network', and it contains the following detail: 'They were executed on 7 April 1944 and buried in the cemetery behind the church, on the outskirts of the town.' Bewilderment. No Resistance network had been uncovered on that date. No one, it seems, had been executed on 7 April that year. The day before, as we know, the Germans had shot the four hostages from L'Echameil. It is unlikely that anyone would confuse these two events. Belonging as they did to old peasant families of the district, the men from L'Echameil were certainly not Jews. Furthermore, a monument in their memory had been erected on the side of road, at the actual site of their murder. I go as quickly as possible to check that this monument bears only the names of the four victims who were killed that day.

The site is much less isolated than back then. The local co-operative has built a large corrugated iron store, painted green, right next to the monument. This is where farmers, do-it-yourself handymen, fishermen, hunters, gardeners, and anybody working with their hands all come to purchase supplies. Among the clientele are many retirees, one of the most active groups within the local population. It is here, beside the building supplies warehouse and the little parking lot, that for the last half century, on 6 April, the annual commemorative ceremony is organised by the ANACR, the biggest of the associations of former Resistance fighters.* French national flags and banners with the hammer and sickle are brought out to flap in the breeze that day. After the speeches, people look around at the numbers present. Each year, there are fewer hands to shake.

The names of the four murdered hostages are also included on the commune's war memorial, listed with the ten other deaths in World War II – for the most part young Resistance fighters in the maquis – alongside the seventy-four names from the 14–18 war, a list that, while immense, is nevertheless still incomplete, and covers three sides of the granite obelisk. It is a bleak monument, lacking any kind of patriotic flourish, like others erected grudgingly by

---

* ANACR – Association Nationale des Anciens Combattants de la Résistance [National Association of Former Resistance Fighters]. This association, in which communists played a significant role, was created soon after the war.

the local councils of this rebellious and essentially pacifist region in the period immediately following the bloodbath of the Great War. Nobody at the *mairie* or anywhere else has any information concerning a fifth person being shot at virtually the same time as the hostages who, while not themselves members of the Resistance, were the parents of resisters and draft dodgers of the STO, and were taken as hostages for that reason. The register of births, deaths and marriages of the commune does not list any violent deaths in April 1944, other than the 'blokes from L'Echameil', as they are usually called. The cemetery – which is not behind the church but on the road leading away from the town, beyond the railway line, nearly a kilometre further on – does not have any grave in the name of Haïm Rozent. Bewilderment then, and even more perplexing in that the letter from Yad Vashem recounts that the three children of this Haïm Rozent, accompanied by their husbands and wife, had made a trip to the country and spent time at their father's grave as recently as 1999. They state with complete confidence: 'We first visited our father's grave and the town where he was murdered, Bugeat.'

Whom did they contact? How have they been able to visit a grave that does not seem to exist? Are they talking about the right place? Have they perhaps mistaken the name of the administrative centre of this canton? Calling it a 'town' when there are only a thousand inhabitants is perhaps an indication that there has been a mistake. There were indeed numerous similar tragedies in this part of the Limousin during the spring of '44. In the so-called 'week of bloodshed' at the beginning of April, dozens of hostages were arrested and several were executed by German soldiers hunting down partisans and Resistance fighters. Every canton has its share of martyrs.

Through my recent research, I have discovered that a round-up of Jews almost always accompanied any military action taken against the Resistance and, while the majority were deported, it seems that some were killed there and then. In his memoirs, Pierre

Trouillé, the prefect of Corrèze who had at that time just taken up his position in Tulle, has drawn up an account of German depredations in the department in April 1944. The sombre balance sheet he produced includes the following figures: 3,000 arrests (of whom 1,500 were kept in confinement), 56 executions by firing squad (*not including Jews*), 100 houses burned to the ground, 300 young men, required for forced labour under the STO, sent to Germany. The business in L'Echameil was far from an isolated case. So, it is not impossible that one tragedy has perhaps been confused with another, especially on the part of foreigners who speak little or no French and are ignorant of both the history and the geography of this remote and secretive part of the country.

The letter from Yad Vashem did not, however, simply describe the pilgrimage undertaken by the children of this mysterious Haïm, of whom it seems nobody here has any recollection: it also contained the broad outlines of his biography, drawn from a witness statement provided by one of his daughters, a statement given in Hebrew and, from what I can gather, tape recorded in Israel and later translated into rather hesitant French.

The story of a man and of a Jewish family caught up in the chaotic madness of the last century. Written on two closely typed, elliptical pages.

My parents were born in Poland and emigrated with their family, each at a different time.

I don't know exactly when our father, Haïm Rozent, arrived in Belgium. What I know now is that his family was very highly regarded in artistic circles and in the theatre and that his mother was an actress in the Yiddish theatre.

My brother [this is a mistake; it should read 'my father'] was born in 1910. He was the director of an orchestra and became a celebrated violinist.

My mother, Mathilda (Malka) Krel, was born in 1916 and arrived in Belgium when she was nine years old, probably shortly after the death of her father. An aunt of my mother was living with her family in Antwerp.

Because of the financial situation, my mother had to go to work almost immediately after her arrival in Belgium. When she was sixteen years old, her feet were causing her such acute pain that she had to have several operations.

My grandmother died of diabetes and my mother, who was then nineteen years old, moved in with my [her?] aunt. In spite of all this sadness, my mother continued to enjoy her youth and she married my father when she was twenty-three years old. The wedding was celebrated in accordance with Jewish religious custom, and this is why my mother kept her maiden name, Krel.

Shortly after my parents' marriage, the Nazis invaded Belgium. My mother, who was pregnant at the time with my older sister, went into exile in Lyon, where my sister was born in May 1940, south of Lyon. Shortly after the birth of my sister, my parents fled again and settled in Sète.

My grandparents had by this time been killed by the Nazis. My parents lived in Sète for two and a half years. I was born there on 21 November 1941.

My name is Hanna (Rosa), and I was named after my maternal grandmother. My mother had miscalculated the time it would take to get to the hospital and this is why I was born at home. At that time, my father was still living with us when he was not involved with his activities in the Resistance.

We have never understood why they had to leave Sète. They fled from village to village and managed to hide with the assistance of the secret army. They sought refuge finally in Tulle. My mother was then pregnant with my brother.

Because of her pregnancy and of the need to stay in hiding, my mother sent my sister and me to stay in a monastery. We have never been able to find out anything about this monastery in spite of numerous efforts.

Even when we were grown up we have not found it easy to talk about the war and the suffering it caused.

In April 1944, when my mother's pregnancy had reached full term (she was expecting my brother) my father was arrested with a number of other members of his Resistance network. They were executed at Bugeat (France) on 7 April 1944 and buried in the cemetery behind the church on the outskirts of the town.

My brother was born at the beginning of May 1944, after the execution of my father. He was named Haïm, after my father.

After the war, in 1945, our mother had some difficulty in getting us released from the monastery where we had been given asylum.

The Jewish Agency and the Haganah took us to Marseille in order to put us on an immigrant ship going to Israel. We had to wait several months in Marseille for the administrative formalities to be completed before we could be embarked. We sailed from Marseille to Naples, where we were transferred to an English ship called *Mataora*. We arrived in Haifa in the middle of June 1945.*

This biographical sketch is so compact and so tangled that it has to be read more than once. But the daughter of Haïm and Malka has not yet finished. She recounts how difficult it was for her mother and her family when they first arrived in the new land that had not yet become Israel. It is evident that Malka disliked the communal

---

* This date is probably a mistake, either of transcription or of memory. The date of arrival may have been June 1946.

living of the kibbutz and that she had a great deal of difficulty adjusting, becoming a proper Israeli at the time the new state was being created. The children, for their part, wanted to forget about the past. 'As children, we wanted to be settled and accepted as soon as possible; this is why, when we came home, we insisted that our mother stop speaking to us in French and use only Hebrew.' She adds this comment: 'There is no need to say how much this decision caused us pain.' This family of Polish origin probably continued to speak the Yiddish of its eastern forebears, but spoke French at home with the children as proof of its integration into Belgian society. When they arrived in Palestine, the children of Malka had to forget the French they had been speaking since their birth, and speaking better and better as they got older. They also had to forget something else. 'In kindergarten, my sister and I used to draw churches and crosses, as we had been taught to do at the monastery, which led to intensive questioning by the other children.' It is easy to imagine the scene she evokes, even in the predominantly secular kibbutzim of that time.

The account also provides some more recent information. Malka, the wife of Haïm, remarried in 1950 and had another child, a daughter called Bluma. Each of the three children born in France during the war has married and had children in their turn. But since the recent death of Malka, there is no one in the extended family who can speak with authority about the past. As in the high country of the Limousin, in Israel too, silence and oblivion threaten to hold sway.

What can be done about this dead man with no grave? Had he really been involved in the Resistance movement in the Haute-Corrèze? Even though he comes from so far away and even though yesterday I did not even know of his existence, I find that I now know more about him than I do about the men from

L'Echameil who were murdered on 6 April, four familiar and
taciturn peasant farmers from the village next to mine. I also
note that Haïm was the same age as my father, that he would
have been ninety years old today, and that he was killed when
he was a little over thirty, the age of my son. My head spins with
these superimposed times.

Minus One

Haute-Corrèze, Autumn 2001–Winter 2002

THE LONG DOCUMENT ON YAD VASHEM LETTERHEAD
ends with some observations from the daughter of Malka
and Haïm that add to my bewilderment and to that of others with
whom I discuss it. She states clearly: 'It was very difficult for us
to see our father's tombstone which has been partly destroyed
due to neglect and the passage of time.' I begin to wonder about
the existence of this strange grave that is not only impossible to
locate but has been eroded by the passing years like a footprint
disappearing into sand.

With none of my usual informants able to help me solve the
mystery of Haïm, it is ultimately a footnote that puts me on the
track again. I find the clue one day when leafing through *The
Maquis of the Corrèze* – a collectively authored book that was
originally published by Éditions Sociales with a preface written
by Jacques Duclos. A copy of the third edition, published in 1975,
had been gathering dust on my bookshelves. In the margin of an

account of the atrocities committed by German soldiers in the Haute-Corrèze on 6 April 1944, a brief footnote provides some information about the fate of the wife of one of the hostages arrested that day:

> Mme Vacher was taken with eleven Jews from Bugeat, brought in by another 'clean-up squad'. She was imprisoned in Limoges, the Jews were deported, minus one, M. Rozent, who was shot dead on the way to L'Église-aux-Bois.

In order to make doubly sure, I consult the fifth and final edition of *The Maquis of the Corrèze* that appeared twenty years later. Supplemented by numerous further witness statements, it has become a weighty volume but it no longer displays the name of any publisher, the publishing firm run by the Communist Party having in the meantime gone out of business. The footnote is still there, this time on page 433, and it has been revised to include a tiny supplementary detail: the name M. Rozent is now followed by his given name, Chaim, a modernised version of Haïm. So, over the course of the last twenty years, we have come to know the dead just a little bit better.

These few lines in tiny print are valuable for more than one reason. They are the only evidence confirming the existence of this Haïm/Chaim of whom nobody around here has any recollection. These few modest words, not considered important enough for inclusion in the main text, confirm at one and the same time that he lived and also the manner of his death. They make me realise the extent to which, several decades after the end of the war, for those involved in the action at the time, one Jew called Chaim among all the others is simply peripheral to the grand story of the nation, the history that matters. The name he has been given is only an estimate. Furthermore, the real point of the footnote is to provide information about the fate of the wife of one of the hostages from L'Echameil, shot on 6 April, for the hostages were fathers of young men in the maquis.

Almost as an aside, there is the casual mention of eleven Jews arrested that day. Eleven: the figure is precise but the people are not named. Eleven shadowy figures. Only their destination is given: Limoges, where each day the gaols run by the Gestapo receive a new batch of temporary detainees. And what then? Complete silence.

I am searching for one man, and now suddenly a whole crowd of strangers has emerged to surround him. I know nothing about them except for the fact that they were arrested on 6 April, Holy Thursday. Their life story begins at its end. Unlike Mme Vacher, who was freed a few months later, these unnamed Jews seem to have disappeared for good. The book about the maquis of Corrèze, written by militant communists on the basis of accounts by former Resistance fighters, does not say whether they survived deportation or whether they died in the camps. The authors, who include many accredited, courageous Resistance fighters, have not thought it necessary to provide this further information. Yet, two decades after the Liberation, so long after the camps were opened, they cannot have been ignorant of the ultimate destination of those people taken by force to Germany. For many years, even among communist sympathisers, reaction to the persecution suffered by Jews was closer to indifference than indignation.

'At the end of the line', as they say in remote areas of the countryside when speaking of electricity or the telephone, comes the reference to the man I have been looking for, the only one to be named – M. Rozent. So, it is eleven 'minus one', to quote the massive book of the Limousin Resistance movement. The phrase could hardly be less informative. Minus one. Now I must try to unravel the mystery of this arithmetic.

✳

I assume that Chaim was probably buried in the cemetery of the neighbouring commune, L'Église-aux-Bois. A death certificate, housed in the archives of the *mairie* at L'Église-aux-Bois, was drawn up after the war and provides immediate confirmation. His body was indeed found where he had been shot, just off the road, on the twisting section of the highway between Ussel and Limoges that runs for several kilometres through one of the least populated communes of the region. A peasant farmer living nearby discovered the body. As the dead man was not a local, as no one was able to identify him immediately, and as the manner of his death made it necessary to proceed with caution, it is likely that his body would have been left for some time lying between the two beech trees, until the proper authorities had been notified. This would explain the discrepancies as to the date of death on several of the official documents. The body was then placed in a temporary grave in the cemetery at L'Église-aux-Bois but only after a woman from the village had brought one of her best linen sheets to serve as a shroud to wrap his body.

I am keen to know more about this Chaim, a violinist who loved Yiddish music, and was finished off by a bullet on the grass verge of a road in the Corrèze. More than half a century late, I long to make his acquaintance.

The cemetery at L'Église-aux-Bois receives very few visitors. The old cemetery adjoins the church, as was the custom almost everywhere in earlier times. Some distance away from any dwellings, church and cemetery are at the centre of a clearing surrounded by steeply sloping fields and protected by trees that form a circular space one might imagine unchanged since the Neolithic period. The first humans to clear land on the Plateau may well have begun around here.

Chaim's grave is immediately obvious, with its rounded top, the Tablets of the Law and Star of David. A Jewish grave cannot pass unnoticed in this part of France! It is no more neglected than other similar graves that are not made of granite. The prevailing humidity has so eroded the two inscriptions placed one above the other, one French, the other Hebrew, that they can only be deciphered with difficulty. In many places I have to put my fingers on the letters and feel the shape, like a blind person reading Braille. It is as though I have found an ancient epigraph, worn away by the action of sand and wind.

In addition to the finding of a court in Tulle in March 1945 that established the identity of Chaim (a photocopy of which I have procured), the *mairie* at L'Église-aux-Bois must have received a request for a permanent burial site which would have provided details regarding the identity of the person who undertook these arrangements on behalf of the deceased man and who decided to erect the tombstone. This must have been shortly after the end of the war, and given the nature of the tombstone, it can only have been people who were close to him, probably members of his own family, beginning with his wife, Malka, and his brother Jacob who had been living with them since their arrival from the south. It was certainly the family who asked for a headstone to be engraved like those in Jewish cemeteries. The result is almost perfect, except for the fact that the curved top has not quite obliterated the broken arch that was customary on Christian graves in earlier times. In front of the headstone, there is a rectangular space filled with white pebbles in the midst of which the ANACR has placed one of the little marble plaques with a tricolour stripe that mark the graves of former Resistance fighters. The ANACR is closely associated with the FTP and I wonder whether, in placing this token of recognition, their intention was simply to pay homage to yet another victim of the Nazis, or was it indeed to honour the memory of a former Resistance fighter? Or was it perhaps both at once?

But what really catches my eye is, in truth, quite a different plaque. Recently placed and quite incongruous, it looks as though it could have fallen from the cabin of an aeroplane or a spacecraft. It is made of aluminium, striking, impervious to the harshness of the climate. Above a text in Hebrew, engraved into the dull metal, a date: 1999. And after the text, a line of Latin characters: 'Chaim Rozent (sûn of Chaim Razen)'. In place of a final signature, two telephone numbers. Over the last few years it has become common to find all sorts of objects placed on graves in order to evoke the memory of the deceased person: sketches, photographs or models of motorcycles, cars, musical instruments, hunting rifles, fishing rods and so on. But it is certainly unusual to find telephone numbers. These have the prefix of a foreign country; it is not difficult to guess which one.

Moved by the discovery of the Jewish tomb, standing alone amidst the others and by the peaceful beauty of the place, I take several photographs of the cemetery, hoping to capture an image of the play of light and shade, the pastures surrounding the crucifixes and columns, the cows that raise their heads from time to time to stare at the intruder. I also take photographs of Chaim's grave. One of them, taken with a telephoto lens, is a close-up of the mysterious aluminium plaque, opening the possibility of communication with the living. As if it were nothing at all unusual, as if the body buried there so long ago wanted to deliver a final message. A message written in a language that the dead man had never spoken because, during his lifetime, Hebrew did not exist as a living language.

Once back in Paris, the photographs, quickly developed and printed, are laid out for a while on a table. I like the reminder of the bold contrasts of the clearing, the soft shadows, the simple strength of the church, the curves of the hillside and of the Jewish tomb. I arrange the best images on a little table and place the table against a wall, so that they will not be far away, so that they will become part of my everyday life, as I try to unravel their secret. There is no hurry.

Then one evening, I pick up the photograph of the aluminium plaque and dial the number. A telephone rings in the night. I do not know where but assume it is in Israel. A woman's voice answers. No, Chaim, the son of Chaim, is not here. He will be back later. You must call back later. No, it is he who will call you.

I ask Eglal, a friend who speaks Hebrew, to serve as intermediary. It feels as though, from the outset, it is not possible to use any language other than the one invented by the Jews of Israel in order to regain their place in the history of the world. A little later that evening, the voice of Chaim speaks from the telephone. He does not hide his emotion. He has been waiting all his life for a call, a call that will wind back time. Something is happening this evening that he no longer believed ever would. He is prepared to spend all night on the telephone, collecting fragments of information about the father who died just before he was born. We abandon Hebrew for English because it is simpler. But his English is worse than mine and it is difficult to find the right words. I speak slowly and reiterate my uncertainties. Every word is highly charged with meaning. Through my hesitant voice, he hears the voice of the father he never knew. How can I meet such feverish, anxious expectations? I am struck by a sudden doubt: should we be stirring up a past such as this? He knows practically nothing about it, and I know little more than he does.

In the next few days, I receive several documents from Israel by email. Among them, a photocopy of a newspaper article. After the Liberation, one of the two Yiddish-language newspapers then published in Paris printed what is in effect a eulogy of Chaim Rozent, senior. I obtain a translation of the article, entitled 'At the grave of a little-known hero'. It was written in Yiddish but printed in Hebrew characters and the photocopy is difficult to decipher due to the lead typeface and poor quality paper in use at the time. It is, however, not simply a conventional obituary.

In April 1944, Nazi murderers encircled the village of Bugeat in the department of Corrèze and they arrested all the Jewish families. They left behind only one Jewish man, Haïm Rozen Wagner, who was severely tortured in order to obtain information about the hiding place of the maquis who were causing the German army serious problems. The Nazi murderers promised Wagner that he would be set free in exchange for the information he provided. Because Rozen, a little-known hero, refused to betray, he was assassinated by the Nazi criminals.

The article continues:

Haïm Rozen, under the name Herman Wagner, is part of a family that is extremely well regarded in the Yiddish theatre. His father, Wagner, was secretary to the Art Theatre of Moscow (Yiddish Kunsttheater) and his mother was a celebrated actress who performed in Poland as well as in Belgium (in Antwerp). She was deported and never returned. His brother, Yekali Rozen Wagner, is well known to audiences of the Yiddish Theatre in Paris.

He was himself an accomplished musician, played the violin, composed, wrote comic sketches and performed on stage. During the Occupation, he organised two dances for the maquis in the Corrèze, and this was why the German murderers arrested him.

After the Liberation, a group of his friends together with local people organised a funeral service and erected a tombstone.

Today, Rozen's widow and his three children, who managed to escape the clutches of the Nazis, live in Israel where they continue the battle for the liberation of the Jewish people. In the name of the Jewish Resistance in

Corrèze, we send her our condolences and the following
message – continue to raise your children in the love of
art and the love of theatre, continue the inheritance of the
Wagner family, which will not be forgotten.

The article, published immediately after the war, does not indulge
unduly in the heroic style that was fashionable at the time. It
reminds readers that Chaim was a well-known and talented artist
and it is this aspect of his life that is commemorated. It does not
say that he was arrested as a member of the Resistance but claims
that he was arrested for having organised two clandestine dances
(the numerical precision here is disturbing). The word 'organised'
raises questions in itself. Would a young musician, used to being
surrounded by music from his childhood onwards and cut off from
it for so long, be able to organise dances without succumbing to
the temptation to play for the young people if handed a fiddle that
was more or less in tune? Did Chaim even still have his own violin
after fleeing so many times and being continually on the move?

The reason for his arrest seems so trivial and inappropriate
that the first translator to whom I gave the article was uncertain
whether she had understood correctly. Slightly troubled, she said,
'I have left out a word there, a word I was not sure about.' The
second translator was bolder and did not hesitate over the motive
for the arrest, however incongruous it may have seemed in relation to what was happening at the time. Yes, it is indeed the word
'dance' that is used, without any other explanation and without
embarrassment in the middle of an article entitled 'At the grave
of a little-known hero'.

In the absence of any other information about the reasons for
the arrest of Chaim, does the claim that he was arrested for having
organised clandestine dances imply that he was the victim of a
denunciation? Did people denounce clandestine musicians? These
dances were, after all, only nominally clandestine because nearly

all the young people of the region used to participate, after having badgered their parents to give consent. Like the police under orders from the Vichy government, the leaders of the Resistance also disapproved of their young fighters indulging in the pleasures of such distractions. Georges Guingouin, the charismatic leader of the FTP maquis and a strong disciplinarian, had shortly before this time severely punished a number of young recruits in his network in Haute-Vienne who were guilty of letting it be known that, for them, going to a dance was more important than security drill and weapon practice.

Extremely popular in rural areas in the last months of the war, these clandestine dances were an insidious and effective form of Resistance to the Occupation. They helped to keep the horrors of the war temporarily at bay both for the young men in the maquis and for many others. Sixty years later, the 'Pearly Nights', a joyful accordion festival that is held at the end of the summer every year in Tulle, still celebrates the role that these dances played in the months before the Liberation. Indeed, it is even claimed that Jean Ségurel, the popular musician from the mountainous region of the Monédières, who enjoyed considerable local fame in the immediate postwar period, played an important role in the struggle against the Occupation because he made the young people dance.

In 1944, when they were unable to catch actual members of the Resistance, German soldiers would often shoot (or burn as at Oradour, or hang as in Tulle) parents or close relatives of the Resistance fighters, among whom it is likely that there were people who frequented clandestine dances and many others who had never done such a thing. But Chaim was not only guilty of frequenting, even perhaps organising, clandestine dances. He was a Jew.

During the period of what was for them the springtime of their last opportunity, the German soldiers threw themselves with renewed vigour into the hunt for Jewish families, hiding here and there throughout the French countryside. At a time when the German army was suffering repeated defeats in one Soviet offensive after the other on the Eastern Front, and rumours were running wild about imminent Allied landings in France, the top priority of the occupying forces in France, under continual harassment by an elusive enemy, was their demented obsession with anti-Semitism and genocide.

On 6 April, having completed their vile task in Bugeat, the SS with their death's head insignia who had accompanied the detachment of the Wehrmacht, left the town in the early afternoon and launched another punitive raid in the neighbouring market town of Tarnac. Unable to flush out any STO draft dodgers or underground fighters, and after discussion with the town clerk (who here, too, was a German-speaking refugee from Lorraine), they took four Jewish men and, as night was falling, they lined them up against the embankment on the road to Nedde and shot them – Henri Dresdner, Wolf Gretzer, Meyer Monheit and Léopold Scheinhaus. The four men, long past their youth, had not thought it necessary to go with their wives and children when they sent them to hide in the woods on hearing the German convoy rumbling around the hairpin bends of the road to Toy-Viam. Their papers were in order, they had been settled in the neighbourhood for several years, they believed they had nothing to fear! Some other Jews – five it seems, women and children – were also arrested in the turmoil and sent off to Limoges. This was still not the end for the little SS detachment, and their sinister cavalcade lasted several more days in the high country of Limousin.

The actions undertaken by the various forces of the Brehmer Division were facilitated by the fact that many Jewish refugees, particularly those who had been accorded French citizenship and had been living in the region for nearly four years, were used to living openly within the local population. Several sent their children to school, not even bothering to disguise their names. They no longer believed that the worst could happen, if they had ever believed it. Many others, the majority, particularly foreigners coming from the south, were simply exhausted by the repeated alerts, by the rumours, true and false. They no longer had the energy to flee, nor the physical strength to spend their nights outdoors in the woods.

Following the lead of the letter from Yad Vashem and the grave at L'Église-aux-Bois, I consult the archives and, with the first documents I open, I begin to realise the extent of the atrocities committed against Jewish people in the Haute-Corrèze during the so-called 'week of bloodshed'. How many people were arrested and deported? Fifty? A hundred? Even more? Around the person of Chaim there is now a swelling crowd of more and more victims, all of them nameless and faceless. Hardly anybody mentions them. Is it possible to identify so many dead people after all this time? Simply to remember that they lived and why they died, so that they can at last find their place in the flow of history.

In the memory of the local people, most of these shadowy figures have long been unidentifiable. As the Jewish refugees were not 'folk from around here', it was very rare for inhabitants of the towns and villages even to know their surnames, let alone to remember them now. They were passing through, they were born in far-off countries, they had multiple family names, gendered patronymics, names you 'couldn't get your tongue around': Pawlowsky, Klocek, Marcinkowski, Abastado, Izbicki, Feldstein, Zampieri… During the Occupation, people were concerned primarily for 'their own' – prisoners of war or STO draft dodgers hiding out in the maquis. They also struggled to provide food for family and friends who did not have the good fortune to live in the country. This of course did not prevent them giving a helping hand on occasion to refugees who were often completely destitute and at greater risk than others. Such assistance was more in the nature of everyday neighbourliness than heroics. Passing on information about an expected police raid, opening a door at the crucial moment could be the difference between life and death for a family. Many people did it. If no local inhabitant has so far been officially recognised as 'Righteous', it is not impossible that someone may yet emerge. There is still time. The numbers of 'Righteous among the Nations' are extremely provisional and have grown from 2,000 to 2,500, then 2,740 and now nearly 3,000, people selected from all over France, whose memory has recently been accorded a place in the Panthéon and celebrated with full republican honours.

Sixty years later, the oldest find their memory failing when I question them about matters they would never dream of raising for themselves. Some people do indeed remember neighbours who disappeared suddenly, abandoning clothes and possessions. Others claim that all the Jews were rounded up at this time and brought to the ballroom at the Café Jabouille. (Before the war, highly successful dances were held there on the afternoons of agricultural fairs, when the business of the day had been completed and the farmers were in no hurry to return home.) But was this the same day? Had there not been other 'round-ups' before this? Reference points are increasingly shaky. There is a memory that emerges hesitantly in many accounts, an image of a group of ten or so women and children, crowded into the back of a military vehicle the day that the 'blokes from L'Echameil' were shot. On that day and not any other. My own questions weigh too heavily on the responses.

The contrast with the meticulous records of the Franco-German administration concerning deportation and camps is striking. Here there is nothing hazy or hesitant. The arrival of prisoners and the departure of convoys to Germany are noted in precise detail at the Drancy prison camp. Thus, we know that on 7 April 1944, twenty-eight people arrived from Limoges. Were the 'eleven minus one', arrested the day before at Bugeat, among the twenty-eight? Could everything have moved so quickly? Could the deportation process have been working so efficiently at a time when it was targeted by railway workers who supported the Resistance and subjected to bombing raids by the Allies? It is more likely that the Jews from Bugeat stayed for several more days in the prison at Limoges before being sent forward to the Paris area. So they probably formed part of another contingent of 133 prisoners from the Limousin who arrived in Drancy on 13 April 1944. I am relying on the fanatical precision of the bureaucrats and executioners in order to find the forgotten victims of Holy Thursday, to identify them. For the moment, I know nothing about them, not even their names.

It would have been a mistake, however, to rely exclusively on these bundles of yellowing paper. Against all expectation, I discover that there are still people of flesh and blood who are concerned about those who died so long before. A letter from the Veterans Affairs ministry arrives at the *mairie* in Bugeat at the beginning of February 2002, requesting that the phrase 'Deceased during deportation' be added to a death certificate issued immediately after the war. Proof positive that, somewhere in the world, someone was taking action in relation to events that had occurred nearly sixty years before. Who is it? While I delve into the administrative documents of a past era, I am galvanised by a new energy. Amazement, relief that I am not the only person in the world concerned about the people who died and whose memory has been buried in the depths of oblivion.

The deportee in question was called Clara Jeanne Uhlmann, née Strauss. She came originally from Liège, was a widow and was then sixty-eight years old, 'last known domicile Bugeat'. She, too, was probably arrested on 6 April 1944 because her name is included in the list of convoys of deportees established by Serge Klarsfeld that I rush to consult. Her death certificate provides the additional information that she died in Auschwitz as early as 4 May. Less than a month after her arrest.

The deceased and the living certainly seem to be in movement at this time, coming more closely together! A few months later, another deceased person – Lucie Fribourg, born in Boulay (Moselle), whose death certificate is similarly preserved at the *mairie* – makes contact from beyond the grave. Her grandson, Henry Fribourg, has been a lecturer in an American university for many years. Recently retired, and in Europe to attend a conference, he and his wife have just been on a sentimental journey to the Corrèze. On the off chance, he left his address, phone number and email address at the bakery. To be drawn to the attention of anyone who might remember his grandmother. One way of saying that the past still has a future. Another bottle thrown into the sea.

Consulting the register of births, deaths and marriages, the mayor finds that the husband of Lucie Fribourg died of an illness several months before the arrest of his wife. The mayor has no difficulty in tracing the family who had rented them an apartment and loses no time in transmitting this information to the American grandson. Although he is himself nearly as old as his grandmother was at the time, the grandson was able to make contact with the former landlady, 'a very elderly lady', he said, living in a retirement home in Paris. She spoke to him about the 'peaceful days' she had spent with his grandmother; she had many memories of her and some keepsakes.

Lucie Fribourg and Clara Uhlmann were at that time two ladies of a certain age, both belonging to the same well-to-do middle class. They had become friends. They must have stayed close to each other in the cramped conditions of the trip to Limoges, shaken and jolted, huddled up against each other in the Wehrmacht truck. After being held for several days in the prison in Limoges, in the section under German control, they were put on the train for Drancy. And then, a few days later, they were in convoy number 72 that left Drancy on 29 April, along with a thousand other deportees, including fifty who came from Corrèze. In the cattle trucks of the special train that waited at the next station, 174 children were crammed among the adults.

Chaim is no longer alone. Two women have joined him. For me, they now have a name and I get into the habit of referring to them, too, by their given names: Lucie, Clara. They are walking at the front of a group that is still anonymous, but it is as though they all belong to the same family.

My interest in Chaim, and in the others around him who came from elsewhere and are now gradually emerging from the shadows, leads me to keep adding more details to the information I have about the beginning of the clandestine struggle in the region. Details about the relations between the two major branches of the local Resistance, the change in attitudes from spring 1943, when many families include a young man hiding out in the maquis, the beginning of armed combat, the ambivalent attitude of the local police later becoming more supportive and so on. There are few survivors from that time, especially among those who were personally involved in the action. So I meet others, those who were on the sidelines, mostly women, who have the great merit in this context of living longer than men. I advance slowly. Nearly all my interviewees tell me they have forgotten everything. For some, this is certainly near the truth. They all, men and women alike, begin by telling me that on this subject no one will ever say anything. I have been warned. As a result, I skirt carefully around the topics that are mentioned only to say we are not going to talk about them: the enthusiasm for Pétain at the beginning, the wait-and-see attitude, the initial reluctance of the communists, the boasting and showing off, the black market, the rivalry between different wings of the Resistance, shaving the heads of women, the settling of scores and summary executions at the Liberation... I have not come to judge or to lay blame. It is too late for that and in any case inappropriate. Besides which, I believe strongly that the behaviour of the population here was by and large more honourable and courageous than in many other places.

I try to explain that all I want is to reconnect with a little bit of the past that has been completely forgotten. Even so, it is not simple. Conversations are halting, focus on absurd details, and either paint a gloomy picture of the difficulties of everyday life at the time or get lost in nostalgic evocations of the good old days, gone forever now, but to which the war had miraculously given a new lease of life. Then the conversation ceases altogether and there is silence. Is this a failure to remember or is it rather the active work of forgetting, more or less deliberately creating a block that cannot be surmounted? There are others, however, especially people I have known for many years, with whom our long friendship means I can dispense with unnecessary hypocrisies and prevarications. I advance by little steps and sometimes great strides.

There is something at once serious and ridiculous, absurd and pathetic in this quest for the final fragments of an old story that will have no repercussions at the national level, in which the community no longer has anything at stake. The history of World War II has been written, specialists look into it from time to time to adjust the overall balance of the picture. I wonder whether the details, so numerous and so painstakingly accumulated by the protectors of memory over so many years, are still important. I tell myself that all this is of no interest to anyone any longer, except myself. And then I remember the children of Chaim and their sleepless nights.

*

I had just begun to find the shadowy trace of the three lost figures – Chaim, Lucie, Clara – when it so happened that I had to
make a brief trip to Israel. One night, I drove in a bus through the
suburbs of Haifa. It was late, well after midnight, but the night sky
was clear and there were lights shining brightly all over the town.
It looked like a successful, wealthy first world city, very different
from the dim lights of the Arab street stalls in Nazareth, where I
had been only an hour before. The children of Chaim, including
Chaim who was named after his murdered father, lived somewhere
in the midst of this profusion of lights and illuminated signs, in
the heart of this modern metropolis that was still pulsing with
life, even though it was the middle of the night. How far this was
from the pitch black nights of the Limousin countryside! I could
feel their presence. I sensed their eager curiosity and even felt I
could hear the sound of their breathing. But I had too little to tell
them, yet perhaps already too much to be able to telephone, to put
it together in haste, call between two flights and arrange to meet
somewhere in a café in Jerusalem. The facts that I knew made a
clumsy package, too ragged and shapeless to be delivered without
explanation. This story belongs to them. It is lying dormant and
perhaps should not be roused too abruptly, and then only with
great care. I did not ask the bus driver to stop and he continued
along the road to Judea. As I looked back one last time at the lights
of Haifa, so Mediterranean, so modern, so confident, so unaware
of the old history of our old countries, I promised myself that as
soon as I got back to France I would hurry to undertake the final
interviews with the last survivors who might yet be able to retrieve
a fragment of their failing memory, and I would immerse myself
in the archives, with all speed, as though there were an emergency.

The Fractured Past

I N ISRAEL, CHAIM, THE SON WHO BEARS THE NAME OF
his murdered father, has taken up residence in the past. His
sisters, Shifra and Hanna, are equally consumed by the story of
the past whose details are as unstable as shifting sand. All three
of them engage in a constant struggle to retain fragmentary or
imagined memories in the hope of bringing others to the surface.

All three were born in France. In different places, due to their
parents' continual need to move house to escape the advancing
German troops and the ever increasing danger: Shifra near Lyon
in 1940, Hanna in Sète in 1941, Chaim in Tulle in 1944. Three
children born on French soil, three children of the war. They
have since discovered that, at the time the first one was being born
in the countryside near Lyon, other members of the family who
had remained in Poland were being killed, one after the other, in
assaults by the *Einsatzgruppen*. At the time the second one was
being born in Sète, their grandmother Elke, who was living with
them, was arrested and deported. When the third was about to

come into this world, their father was slaughtered on a road in the Limousin mountains. For them, birth has always gone hand in hand with death.

They told me they had left France and emigrated to Palestine early in the summer of 1945. They went with their mother by sea from Marseille. At that time there were few civilian ships and it was far from easy to book a passage, especially to go to that part of the world. They managed to get in ahead of the crowds that later packed into the *Exodus* – which would not embark from Sète until 1947 – and all the other hastily improvised vessels transporting the flood of people who would establish and populate the future state of Israel. The exhausting journey inevitably became a new exodus and, for the children, an epic experience. Even though they were very young, have they ever forgotten the pushing and shoving, the anxiety, the dazzling light, the sea wind and the taste of salt on their lips? Or the dark shadows of the shattered buildings in the Vieux Port, destroyed by German bombardments, the shape of the Pharo lighthouse dominating the entrance to the channel? The ship on which they embarked from Marseille did not go directly to Palestine, but took them to Naples, where they were transferred to an English vessel that was to deliver them finally to a place of refuge, a country that as yet had no name, where fighting was still occurring sporadically, and where the British soldiers were often as intimidating as the militant Arabs.

Once settled there, the children continued to speak French but, over time, they must, of necessity, have forgotten their French. Their lives had begun in France, but then they must have forgotten France. In order to survive, they had to invent a new life, a life that at that stage had no past. For many years, within the family, the war was never mentioned and they never spoke about France. *Black out.** They did, however, continue to talk with pride and

---

* In English in the original. [Note from the translator]

respect about their dead father, a hero from another world and another time.

It was so different for us, children born here in France who have never known separation or exile. The exhilarating sight of a disorganised group of retreating German infantrymen, glimpsed cautiously from behind a curtain, is an image that still haunts the dreams of French children born, as I was, just before or in the first year of the war. Memorialising those events and the emotions of the time is a task in which many have shared.

Parents and schoolteachers, newspapers, films and books and the first comic strips continued throughout our childhood to tell the same story, to create the same image whether at the private level of family memory or in the official press: a defeated army, heroic young members of the Resistance, ecstatically happy crowds, barricaded streets in liberated Paris, tricolour flags hastily sewn together by mothers and grandmothers using strips of fabric found in attics, the figure of General de Gaulle against a triumphantly blue sky, the bright smiles of American soldiers riding in their tanks. Whenever these stopped anywhere on a poplar-lined highway in the Île-de-France, members of the tank crew would pick up children, hold them in their arms, give them an orange – the first the children had ever seen. Small children, thus, also played their part in the Liberation, always written with a proud capital letter. I still have the photographs taken by my parents. Many years later I actually met an elderly American, revisiting Europe, who insisted he could recognise himself in these snapshots, standing next to me, a little boy in his Sunday best with his hair neatly combed, perched on the turret of a tank between two laughing Yankee soldiers. For the grown-ups it was a time of immense relief, a historic redemption. For the children of France, it was a festival, a time of jubilant celebration but also the beginning of a fantasy that continues to this day.

For the children of Malka, so young, so vulnerable, there was nothing like this. For them, history stopped during the long, slow months (more than a year) between the death of their father and their departure for Palestine. What did the defeat of Nazism mean to them? Were they able to gauge the decreasing level of threat? Did they experience the way the liberated population began to breathe again, rediscovering its natural rhythm? Did they see the euphoric processions of swashbuckling Resistance fighters, parading along the streets of Tulle, or the little groups that formed around collaborators and suspected traitors, encircling them in pools of hatred? The shadow cast by the bodies of murdered hostages, hanged by the German soldiers from balconies, lamp posts and from butchers' hooks, darkened the mood of the town. Their mother must have held their hands tightly and told them to keep their eyes down and, above all, not to look back when they came across a crowd of emotional people. When they arrived in Marseille, did they have to make their way through yet more joyous, patriotic celebrations as they left the St Charles station? I offer them these stereotypical images that seem to stir no memories for them.

But they cannot stop poring over the photograph of their parents, posing in front of a wrought iron gate, the only irrefutable image of that period of the war that they have obtained (see Plate 14). It was almost certainly taken in the Limousin. I examine it in my turn, to see if I can recognise the design of the gate, the curve of the hillside, find some trace of a familiar landscape. Dressed in warm clothing, the parents are each holding a child in their arms. The photograph provides no further information about what it shows: it is winter, probably early in 1943, soon after their arrival on the Plateau. There is a hint of some pine trees and a few houses in the background. The family looks happy, serious and happy. The photograph tells us nothing of the distress, the constant alarms, and nothing about what will follow.

*

Many years later, as soon as the children of Chaim, the 'little-known hero', had themselves become parents, they became obsessed with a single idea: to return to France, to discover what they could about their fractured past, to try to put the pieces together again. To rediscover the France of their origins, the place where their happiness was destroyed and where the unity of the family was lost, precisely the place where the photograph was taken. To find out where their father was buried. To clear up the mystery surrounding his death and their mother's desperate flight.

For her part, their mother remained stubbornly silent. She refused to share the memories that weighed so heavily on her. She developed the habit of deflecting the speaker whenever the subject arose in conversation. The least reference to that past experience stirred deep and painful emotions in her and her skill and persistence in changing the subject became an automatic, natural reflex.

And so an invented or imagined story became the family's official history. Made up of fragments, it could be told in a few words. Did the children ever suspect that it was too simple, too admirable? Probably not at the beginning and perhaps not even now.

Only once did their mother give them her version of the period of the war in France, an account that sounds like a devotional tale. It can be summarised as follows:

While we were living by the sea in Sète, a town in the south of France, your father left us to join the Resistance in a remote part of the country. Where he went, there were mountains and forests. Precisely because of these mountains and forests, the Resistance fighters were more numerous and better organised than elsewhere. That country was called Corrèze. It was there, in a village whose name I can tell you (she spelled out the name carefully because of its strange French sounds), that he became one of the leaders of the local Resistance and was captured by the Germans

along with other Resistance fighters. They were found and
all of them were shot. Your father is buried in the village
cemetery. After the war, his comrades in the Resistance,
Jews, paid homage to him in a remarkable article that was
published in Paris in a Yiddish newspaper.

And she preserved the precious newspaper clipping as carefully
as though it were an exhibit in a court of law.

The other half of the story was the parallel account of her life
at the same time:

While Chaim was fighting in the Resistance, I moved so
that I could be closer to him. I left the south of France and
settled with Shifra and Hanna in a little town that is the
capital of Corrèze. When my husband died, I was in hospital due to my pregnancy. This was in the spring of 1944
and I was about to give birth. I was able to entrust the two
little girls to some nuns in a convent.

Notwithstanding the fact that a significant number of clergy tol-
erated and even condoned the Vichy administration, there were
also many Catholic and Protestant schools and other religious
establishments that served in effect as refuges for Jewish children.
But Malka often used to tell her daughters how she had had great
difficulty after the war in reclaiming them, the nuns presumably
reluctant to let go of these young Jewish souls that had so recently
and so providentially been accepted into the bosom of the Church,
albeit without their knowledge. It is almost certain that the two
children were baptised and it is now known that French clergy
had been advised by the Vatican to try to avoid returning to their
Jewish families children who had been sheltered and baptised.
At least one letter, admonishing the Apostolic Nuncio in Paris
in relation to this advice, was leaked from the Vatican's secret

archives in 1946. It was common knowledge that the nuncio, Monsignor Roncalli (the future Pope John XXIII), disagreed with the policy advocated by Pope Pius XII in relation to the retention of Jewish children. The policy amounted in effect to a process of spiritual kidnapping, inflicted on the young by the institutions of the Catholic Church, with the blessing of the Pope.

The episode of the convent haunted the dreams of the children into their adult life, and perhaps awakened in them some atavistic fears in relation to Christians, a whiff of the pogrom that Jewish families originating in Poland carry deep within themselves. Many years later, in Israel, one of Malka's daughters was determined to uncover the mystery of her earliest childhood. She boldly resorted to hypnosis to attempt to find out more about this repressed and obliterated past. She told me of her utter amazement. In a convent, a winged angel came to her and in a low voice told her about the death of her father. She saw him, heard him speak. So notwithstanding the grave in the cemetery in Corrèze and thanks to her, their father still lives.

And then one day, the three children, now grown up, accompanied by their husbands and wife, decided to visit the region where their father had been killed and where his body was buried. It was more than fifty years since the end of the war and they were themselves well into their fifties. They were considerably older than their father had been at the time of his death. Their mother, who had not wanted them to remember, or who had perhaps been afraid to dig up the past, had just died. Her death liberated them and they thought the time had come for them to try to find out more about what had happened.

It was the last, or the next to last, summer of the century. They mingled with the normal holidaymakers whom they resembled in terms of their clothes, their sunglasses and their cameras. But not with respect to their accent. It is rare indeed, even in the summer months, to hear Hebrew spoken on the Plateau. However, they had no problem communicating with local tradespeople, using English and the kind of pidgin that has developed in recent years as increasing numbers of English and Dutch people have bought houses in the region.

The first place they went to was the war memorial. It comes as no surprise to hear that they had some difficulty finding it, as the memorial has been frequently on the move since it was first erected in 1922. Despite its massive bulk, it was relocated from its original site in one of the main squares of the town, firstly to the new cemetery, and subsequently to the showground, where it is still standing today. In the depopulated country areas of France, the dead draw attention to themselves more insistently than elsewhere. Our Israeli tourists scanned the names of the seventy-four soldiers killed during World War I, then the ten or so from World War II and the two from the Algerian War. So many names but no Rozent! Mystification, stupefaction. 'And yet he really was a member of the Resistance!' 'But he wasn't French. Could French war memorials be reserved for the French?' This was a reasonable supposition given the litany of names of the victims of the two world wars incised into the granite monument: virtually all the surnames of the victims are those of local families. Until very recently, there were few incomers to this part of the country.

The three children took photographs of themselves standing in front of the memorial that failed to commemorate their father. It was a beautiful day, they looked happy, more like tourists than pilgrims, ordinary tourists in front of an ordinary war memorial that had nothing to do with them. Were there perhaps other memorial sites in this town that was so close to their hearts and yet so alien? They strolled along the main street, a street that resembles thousands of other equally unremarkable main streets connecting, organising and dividing the little towns of the Massif Central. Their mother had given them no details, no landmark that could have helped them to orient themselves. To whom could they turn for advice? It would make sense to speak to some of the older inhabitants but then what would they ask? How would they be able to pick former members of the Resistance? In the end they left with nothing, having found not the slightest trace of the life or the death of their father.

But there remained the grave. That, at least, did still exist, the only tangible proof of that faraway tragedy. They were able to find the grave, located some ten kilometres away, following the instructions their mother had left. They had brought with them the snapshot, dating from the months immediately following the end of the war, in which she had asked to be photographed standing beside the headstone that marked her husband's grave.

So it was that the children of Chaim, continuing their search for memories, made their way towards the aptly named L'Église-aux-Bois [Church-in-the-Wood]. Pale with emotion but also profoundly happy, they discovered a landscape that Caspar David Friedrich might have painted: a wide clearing in thickly wooded countryside, the trees with dark and light foliage, the church and graveyard precisely located at the centre of the clearing, surrounded by pastures in which were grazing Limousin cows with their distinctive golden-red colouring. Everlasting peace and serenity, virtual absence of fear. The little group from Israel was struck first by the profusion of greens in the landscape, by the thick shade of the pine plantations they traversed before emerging into the clearing, by the brilliance of the lush pasture, by the play of light in the foliage of the huge beech trees around the edge of the field. People who have lived for decades in the suburbs of Haifa where, on the days when the khamsin blows, everything is enveloped in powdery dust, marvel at the absence of stones, and exclaim that everything is so green, there is so much water, the air is so brilliantly clear as far as the eye can see. The solitude also came as a surprise for there was no sign of human life in the whole expanse of the clearing. The grave where their father is lying seemed to belong to a different world. The bolt on the iron gate of the graveyard clanged behind them and the hinges grated. There were no other sounds apart from the gravel crunching beneath their feet, and high above them the comforting drone of an aeroplane.

The grave is utterly mystifying for anyone not aware of the circumstances of Chaim's death. It is the only one of its kind in the graveyard and one of the very few in existence that can bear witness to the attempted extermination of the Jewish people by the Nazi regime, because the vast majority of the 6 million victims of the Shoah have no grave, their bodies were sublimated from the earth. Their executioners managed to get rid of virtually all trace of their final suffering and their murder. The Nazis tried obsessively to remove these traces and they almost succeeded, which is another way of saying that in the end they failed.

So Chaim's grave in a corner of the cemetery in L'Église-aux-Bois is an exception, one of only a thousand or so scattered here and there across the whole country. At the heart of this quiet countryside, where trees are far more numerous than people, is an immense invisible throng, the crowd of the unburied dead. The lonely grave may be simple and modest but it constitutes an important sign, marking the ground itself, and it continues to trouble the conscience of the living. Visitors are welcome to come and place a stone on the grave, according to Jewish custom.

Before leaving Israel, Chaim's children had designed an aluminium plaque on which was engraved a text in Hebrew and some telephone numbers. Finally giving up hope of finding anyone to whom they could talk, they stuck the plaque into the gravel that covers the grave. Like a classified advertisement appealing for the rest of time to any passers-by who might venture as far as this remote graveyard. Those who can read Hebrew will see from the statement that the children of the deceased – who 'was a member of the Resistance' and 'was killed in the prime of his life' – wish, by means of this plaque, to honour his memory and that of their mother, who had died in Israel a few years earlier. Anyone who wished to do so was urged to telephone one of the numbers. Not to seek further information but if possible to provide it.

The little advertisement, with its precise date in 1999, did indeed fulfil its role of bottle thrown into the ocean. The telephone rang in Haifa several months later. And the past resurfaced, like a cork bobbing up in the water.

Jem

O N SEVERAL OCCASIONS, IN THE COURSE OF THE inconclusive conversations I initiated, a fleeting memory would surface of a young man who had been active in the town during the war. Known by many, liked by all, his name was Jem. I was intrigued by the name because it was unusual in a region where there are relatively few surnames and these are therefore readily identifiable, and where given names tend to be traditional. In this community, until quite recently, men were called after their fathers and grandfathers, Léonard, Antoine, Jean, Pierre, Joseph, François, Louis, Jules, Jacques... Léonard was for a long time one of the most common, due to the adoption of that benevolent figure as the patron saint of the Limousin.

Nor did Jem sound like one of the nicknames which young people in the country used to bestow on each other that would often remain attached to them for the rest of their life. The pronunciation and spelling suggested an Anglo-Saxon name. But was it not rather an alias such as those assumed as a precaution, and sometimes out of affection, by members of the Resistance, to disguise their real identity? But the man who bore this name had no other claim to fame, according to my informants, than to have worked as an assistant to one of the four barbers in the town.

Then one day, when the name of Jem arose yet again in the course of a conversation, I recalled the letter written by Yad Vashem to the Rozent family. Could it possibly be that the Chaim Rozent who was killed by the Germans and seemed to have left no trace in the memory of anyone in the town, and the assistant barber were one and the same person? In his place of work he was known simply as Jem. The name served as both family name and given name; it was discreet, easy to remember, and it was a rough phonetic transcription of Chaim. Had he adopted this name when he arrived in Corrèze? Was he perhaps already using it in Belgium and in the south of France so that no one would be led inopportunely to the unusual biblical name of Chaim, rendered somewhat ridiculous in French by a soft initial consonant? Chaim is neither David nor Jacob. During the war nobody knew Chaim, but many were acquainted with Jem.

I immediately seek to interview the widow of the barber who had employed him. After the death of her husband, she had set up a business selling cosmetics, haberdashery and children's clothes in the former barber's shop. One of those brave, frivolous enterprises that attempt in a modest way to follow the fashions set in the big towns while ignoring modern notions of profitability, a shop like so many in small country towns before mass ownership of motor cars and the invention of the mega shopping mall.

We begin by talking about the weather, the end of season warmth which has given such a boost to business, of the temperature that falls dramatically at night. It has begun to get cold since yesterday. One can feel the onset of winter. She has never heard of Chaim, nor of Rozent, absolutely not. But, on the other hand,

1. View of Bugeat around the middle of the twentieth century.

2. Bugeat today, the church and *mairie* (formerly the boys' school) in the centre of the village. The school was requisitioned by the German army as their headquarters during their week-long occupation of the village in April 1944.

3. The Grand Hôtel de Paris in Bugeat (Chaim was arrested by German soldiers on the square in front of this hotel on 6 April 1944).

4. Church and cemetery at L'Église-aux-Bois.

5. Plaque on Chaim Rozent's grave in the cemetery at L'Église-aux-Bois.

The top panel reads: PN [*po nitman, 'here lies'*] Chaim Son of Ben-Zion Razen, who was killed by the Nazis in his youth (age thirty-four) on the sixth day [*Friday*], thirteenth of Nisan, Taf Shin Dalet, corresponding to 7/4/1944, and who was buried on the first day [*Sunday*], fifteenth of Nisan, Taf Shin Dalet

T.N.Z.B.Ha

[*tehe nishmato ʒrurah beʒror ha'haim, 'May his soul be attached to the living'*]

The lower panel reads: This plaque was affixed in May 1999 in the memory of Chaim and the memory of his wife Malka, daughter of Isaac, who died on the nineteenth of Nisan, Taf Shin Mem Het, corresponding to 6/4/1988, and who was buried in Israel. T.N.B.Z.Ha

This plaque was affixed by the children of Chaim and Malka: Shifra, Hanna, Chaim and Bluma, and also their families living in Israel.

ISRAEL
Chaim Rozent (son of Chaim Razen)

[*Translation from the Hebrew and explanations in italics by Joel Rosen*]

On the gravestone:

ICI- REPOSE
~~ROZENT~~ ~~CHAIM~~
FUSILLÉ PAR
LES ALLEMANDS
LE 7.4.1944
À L'AGE DE
34 ANS

6. Malka Rozent with neighbours and friends at the grave of her husband in L'Église-aux-Bois, 1945. (Photograph found in papers belonging to M. Beynat, who is standing on the right.)

7. Handwritten inscription from Malka on back of this photograph, reading:
'To all my dear friends, as an everlasting reminder of our friendship during the
war of 1940–45, I offer you this photo of the grave of my poor husband. I am
forever devoted to you all. Marie Rozent. Pérols s/Vézère, 21 June 1945.'

8. Lucie Fribourg, arrested in Bugeat on 6 April 1944, and her husband Albert, who had died in Bugeat the year before.

9. Carola Hoch, arrested in Bugeat on 6 April 1944, and her son (wearing the uniform of the conscripted youth workers).

10. André Drouaine (right), Bugeat 1943, a construction worker on the Vézère dam who passed on messages for the Resistance, was deported and died in Germany in January 1945.

11. Studio portrait of
Chaim Rozent, probably
taken in Antwerp
before the war.

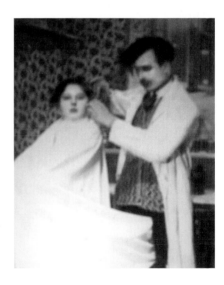

12. Chaim Rozent working
as a hairdresser, probably
in Antwerp before the war.

13. Chaim playing his violin at a fund-raising event in Antwerp, probably in 1936.

14. Chaim and Malka (right) Rozent with their daughters, Shifra and Hanna, and an unknown woman (centre), probably taken in Limoges in 1943.

15. Malka Rozent (right) with her children, Shifra, Hanna and Chaim. Photograph probably taken in Pérols in the spring of 1945.

16. Group of Resistance fighters from Bugeat and surrounding villages, 1944 (back row, second from left Roger Chalat, third from left Emile Larivière).

17. Parade of Resistance fighters, Bugeat 1944.

En mémoire des victimes du nazisme
arrêtées à Bugeat pendant la guerre 39-45

Lucie FRIBOURG, 71 ans, morte à Auschwitz
André DROUAINE, 20 ans, mort à Königstein
Brana TENCER, 38 ans, morte à Auschwitz
Serge TENCER, 3 ans et demi, mort à Auschwitz
Chaïm ROZENT, 33 ans, mort à l'Église-aux-Bois
Carola HOCH, 49 ans, morte à Auschwitz
Clara UHLMANN, 68 ans, morte à Auschwitz
Anna KLEINBERG, 11 ans, morte à Auschwitz
Rosa KLEINBERG, 9 ans, morte à Auschwitz
Maryem KLEINBERG, 41 ans, morte à Auschwitz
Anna IZBICKA, 6 ans, morte à Auschwitz
Jeanne IZBICKA, 16 ans, déportée à Auschwitz

18. Plaque on wall of *mairie* in Bugeat. 'To the memory of the victims of Nazism arrested in Bugeat during the '39–'45 war'.

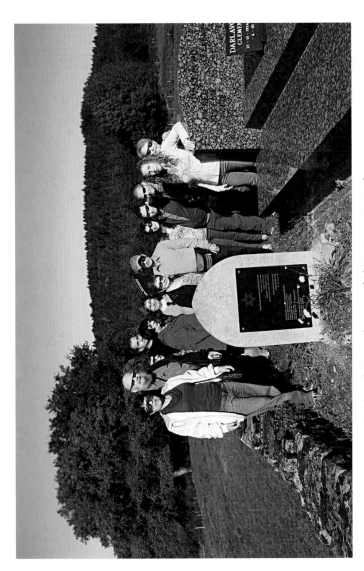

19. Family gathering at the grave of Chaim Rozent, September 2015.

she has clear memories of Jem, 'a very nice young man and a good barber'. Behind her, pots are boiling on the kitchen stove and I can feel my cheeks burning with the heat. I accept with alacrity the drink she kindly offers me.

She cannot recall that period without constantly returning to the fear which is still vivid in her memory:

> Everyone knew my husband worked for the Resistance. We were never betrayed but we were afraid all the time. And then there were the German convoys that, at that time, went right past our window, which threw us each time into the same terror.

As always, when people think back to that period of the Occupation, the strongest memories are the pervasive fear and then wonder at the fact that they were never denounced, even though at the beginning of the war several of the shopkeepers had set up in pride of place next to their cash registers little collection boxes adorned with an image of Marshal Pétain.

She remembers Jem's family, his wife and two little girls: she says they lived in a small house further up the hill on the Rue Nationale.

> I lent his wife a pushchair and also a perambulator. Wasn't she expecting another baby? In any case, she disappeared overnight the day they arrested her husband. I would have really loved to know what became of them. Things were hard for everyone at that time. For them too, of course. You know, we helped them a great deal.

I ask her about the role played by Jem in the Resistance and she is utterly mystified. As far as she knows, he had had nothing to do with the Resistance. He had been employed by her husband, who had given him a job because, at that time, the town and all the villages for miles around were bursting at the seams, there was a great deal of work for the barbers, hair to be cut, beards to be trimmed, faces to be shaved. No, the Resistance didn't come into it at all.

Just when the jigsaw seemed almost complete, suddenly the final pieces fail to fit. So many questions arise. Had Jem perhaps not been a member of the Resistance as imagined by his family and friends? Why had Malka, his wife, hidden from her two daughters that she had shared the final days of their father's life, right up until the morning when he left for work, doubtless promising as usual to be back early, that day when he never returned? Why had she invented the story of setting up house far away from him? Was it in order to avoid having to talk about such painful memories? Strategic avoidance or amnesia?

Our memories erase at least as much as they retain of the past, as I have frequently found in my own life. Every attempt to recreate the past is like the early journeys of discovery in which, the further the explorers went, the more aware they became of the vast extent of the unknown, the areas left white on their maps.

A question that puzzled me is how a professional musician could also be a competent barber... The issue may seem of secondary importance, perhaps even slightly absurd, but it should not be dismissed out of hand. Because being a barber, contrary to popular belief, is not a skill that can be learned overnight. René, my mother's brother, was a barber. He had learned his trade in Paris and spoke of it with pride. During the war, he came back home to the country and opened a salon at the bottom of the high street. He paid as much attention to the proper cutting of hair, the elegance of his own attire and the graceful manipulation of his Bakelite cigarette holder as he did to the skill of trout fishing. He had the sunny face and the withdrawn look in his eyes of those who are destined to die young. As a child, I admired him enormously. There is no way he and Jem would not have met each other. I imagine them sitting on the terrace at the Hôtel Panet, on a Sunday evening in summer, deep in a discussion that perhaps never took place.

At this stage in my fantasising, I discover that Jem was by no means a novice or untrained barber. Before the war, in Antwerp, he had already worked in a hairdressing salon in order to supplement his income, music providing an unreliable living.

Although he was indeed a barber by trade, Jem would only have been taken on by his future employer after certain enquiries had been made, given the nature of the latter's other activities and the risks they posed for himself and his relatives. The barber was in effect one of the people known among the members of the Resistance as 'legals', in other words someone who worked for the Resistance without going underground. Living a normal life in the community, their task was to maintain communications with the maquis, to pass on instructions, to warn of impending danger and, at night, to organise the supply of food. As a result, the 'legals' were more exposed than the Resistance fighters themselves, who spent their days hiding in the woods. It is likely that the barber sounded Jem out, exchanging some careful general remarks, between two clients, and he had perhaps discovered that Jem's family based in eastern Europe were long-standing members of the old socialist party, affiliated with the *Bund*. That connection would not, however, have been anything like a sufficient credential to have permitted Jem to join the Resistance or be accepted without suspicion. Furthermore, as a young Jewish refugee, under police surveillance,[1] with no income or local support network, surely his first concern would have been to protect his pregnant wife and his two children?

Unanswerable questions keep arising. At this point, archival research comes to the rescue and provides a measure of certainty. The pages covered with old-fashioned handwriting are

unequivocal concerning many details about life at that time that
have been completely erased from the memories of the oldest
inhabitants. Not life as imagined or dreamed, but real life. The
question as to what brought Jem to the Haute-Corrèze during
the winter of 1942–3 receives a simple answer, both political and
administrative: when the Germans took over the unoccupied
zone, they moved immediately to evacuate from the coastal areas
of the Mediterranean all the foreign Jews who had fled there and,
for reasons that remain obscure, to direct those refugees who had
been living in the departments of Aude and Hérault to go to the
Massif Central. Jem was one of those.

Hounded out of Sète, he was taken to Rodez and put on a
special train that, at dusk on a freezing cold day in early January,
stopped at one little station after another along the Limousin
Mountain line to unload its cargo of foreign Jewish refugees.
Together with his wife, the two little girls and his brother Jacob,
he lived first in the market town of Pérols, where the train had
dropped them and where accommodation had been rapidly
requisitioned. He was immediately conscripted into the 151st
GTE,* one of the work camps established by the Vichy regime
with the aim of simultaneously supervising, controlling and
exploiting the large numbers of foreigners from many nations
now scattered throughout the country. Jem had little choice in
the matter: in order to provide for his family he learned how to
use a spade to work in the peat bogs. The (relative!) efficiency of
peat as a source of heating fuel had recently been rediscovered,
and since the beginning of the war, the extraction of peat from
the moorland around Pérols and Saint-Merd-les-Oussines had
once again become a major industry. It is highly likely though,
that as Jem was of a slim build and rather delicate, he would not
excel in a task requiring physical strength and the ability to work
outdoors in all weathers.

---

* Groupement de Travailleurs Étrangers [Foreign Workers' Brigade].

It was seven months later, in August 1943, that he was drafted by the group commander to the barber in the main town of the canton, after the latter let it be known he needed an assistant and was looking for a qualified barber. Jem was thus assigned the role of barber's assistant, employed in the commercial centre of the town, an inhabitant on almost the same footing as anyone else. This period of relative peace and security did not last long. As early as September he was summoned to Tulle for an obligatory medical examination. I have the official documents relating to this summons before my eyes now, the references to Jem are scanty and repetitive. It seems that, like so many other Jews in the same situation, Jem did not answer the summons, doubtless fearing that it was a trap, a prelude to deportation, the subject that haunted so many anxious, whispered conversations. He disappeared for more than two months. This means he was classified as 'recalcitrant' or a 'defaulter', according to the terms in use at the time; he was certainly in breach of the law, liable to be severely punished as a deserter, all the Jews forcibly evacuated from the south having been effectively placed under house arrest. The police investigating his whereabouts interviewed his neighbours and, of course, his wife. Malka's response to police questioning reveals what she did in fact fear: 'I was waiting to hear from him as I suspected he had been drafted to work in the occupied zone.' Did he seek refuge in the maquis during the period of his flight? This hypothesis cannot be ruled out, given the key role of places such as the barber shop where he worked in relation to the FTP branch of the Resistance. But there is no clear evidence to indicate that this did happen. The yellowing pages of the reports I scan reveal only an occasional fragment of information. And for obvious reasons there is no information at all about underground activities.

Jem reappears early in the New Year in 1944, he goes back to work in the barber's shop and moves house from Pérols to Bugeat, where he settles with his wife, his two young daughters and his brother Jacob, who is working in a factory making wooden clogs and sabots: once the French army stopped buying harnesses for the cavalry, effectively the town's only export industry was the manufacture of wooden-soled shoes and clogs, dispatched by the wagonload from the local railway station. Jacob, who had taken the name Jacques, was greatly appreciated by his employers for his skill in leather work. Events had not been able to separate the two brothers: in Belgium they gave concerts and played together for dances and balls, each in his own way. Jacob was not only an instrumentalist but also an accomplished tap dancer. After having traversed the whole of the country from the north to the south, they thank heaven that they are still together in this final place of refuge.

Jem is happy to be back at work, among people with whom he is at ease, in a country that has been re-energised since the outbreak of the war due to the coming and going of legions of French and foreign refugees as well as the workers employed on the construction of the dam on the river Vézère. He does not stay hidden in the salon. He is often to be seen in the street on his way to people's homes to cut hair or shave the beards of invalids. The locals like to stop and chat with him because he is young, lively, discreet and kind, and because word has got around that he was a professional musician and that rouses people's curiosity.

At this time the Resistance begins to step up the pressure all over the country, mounting more and more daring attacks. This night-time violence, more for show than to inflict real damage, worries some people but provides reassurance to many others who start to hope again. That must also be the case for Jem. Fear begins at last to recede. The fear that had led him into hiding to avoid the round-ups and other underhand tricks perpetrated by the Vichy regime. He never stops thinking about the arrest of his mother, a few months earlier in Sète. The fear is long-standing and deeply rooted: from the moment of their arrival in the region, he and Malka took the painful decision to separate themselves from their two young daughters. Judging that the children would be safer and better cared for in town than in the country, they had placed them in a children's home in Limoges called La Pouponnière [The Nursery], set up to provide refuge for Jewish children. While there, Shifra's name was changed to Sylvia, and Hanna's to Anna. On several occasions during the course of 1943, the parents must have taken the train and gone to visit their children. It was probably on one of these visits that the precious photograph was taken that is now preserved with such care in the family photograph album in Haifa. That photograph, the only one. I gaze at it again, just as they gazed at the camera. Each parent, carrying one of the children, concentrating so as to lose nothing of the moment of happiness. In the middle of the scene, there is an unknown woman, doubtless the wife of the man who was taking the photograph (in those days it always used to be the men who took the photographs) and she, too, is gazing fixedly at the camera. Everyone seems to sense the importance of the moment. Malka has the hint of a smile; Jem is carrying the older daughter, dressed in her best clothes, a white ribbon in her hair, and he has the serious expression men tend to adopt at moments of pride.

In Limoges they must have been relieved to discover that a number of Jewish institutions were still managing to survive, due to determination, ingenuity and skill at negotiation, and that the little rabbinical seminary was even able to continue teaching. The children's boarding house was discreetly located in the grounds of a beautiful and substantial house dating from the beginning of the century, 46 Rue Eugène-Varlin, in the suburb overlooking the left bank of the river Vienne. The two little girls would stay at La Pouponnière until it was suddenly closed down, the day after Christmas Day 1943, when the fifty or so babies and toddlers who were still there were either returned to their parents, or hastily evacuated and placed in temporary refuges by the OSE (Oeuvre de Secours aux Enfants – an organisation for the rescue of Jewish children).

Malka and Jem had sought to protect that which was most precious to them from the widespread dangers that they felt to be imminent. Every day they wondered if they had made the right decision. They thought of the other members of their family who had stayed in Poland, or who were scattered in other parts of Europe. They could not have imagined that every one of them had been exterminated, that they were now alone in the world, perhaps the sole survivors of their line. Warned on Christmas Day by staff from the OSE, they made a dash to Limoges and picked up their two little daughters.

At the beginning of 1944, the family was thus reunited once again. Malka was pregnant for a third time. The Resistance fighters in the Limousin were becoming more and more daring, rumours were spreading about an impending Allied landing, the war was coming to an end. There was a ray of light shining through the window, happiness was no longer forbidden. That was the moment when Jem agreed to participate in the organisation of the first clandestine dance.

This long-dead man has become a real person to me, a person whose life story I am beginning to discover, whose face is almost familiar and now I find that he has not finished springing surprises on me. Just next to the *mairie* in the neighbouring town of Lacelle, located in recent years in what used to be the school, I discover a plaque made of blue-veined granite, one of those that are very common in the region, on which has been engraved a list of names intended to catch the attention of passers-by. In the event, although it has clearly been installed only recently, the fact that it is lying flat on the ground at a bend in the road means it is unlikely to be noticed by many! I had myself passed by on numerous occasions without seeing it. If I find it today, it is because I am looking for it, because I have heard about its existence, because I am told I will find on it the names of the Jewish children arrested in the town's school at the beginning of the 'week of bloodshed', on 4 April to be precise, two days before Holy Thursday. And there they are at the bottom of the memorial, these children listed with their name and their age, the family name before the given name just like when the schoolteacher calls the register in the morning assembly:

Muller Georgette 6 years, Wais Irène 7 years, Szerman Sonia 9 years, Buchner Roseline 10 years, Wais Monique 10 years, Muller Jacqueline 14 years.

Among the six, two sisters from two families. When they were taken, the four of them must have walked together hand in hand.

I look higher. In the middle of the list of adult martyrs, I see another Szerman. This one was twenty-five, he was called Ferdinand and was probably the brother or cousin of little Sonia. This Szerman was shot like Jem, perhaps she even saw his body fall as the bullets hit home. She was nine years old. She had been arrested because she was Jewish. Why did Ferdinand Szerman suffer a different fate? Because he was a man? In Tarnac, as in a number of neighbouring places during the course of that month of April, men were shot while women and children were taken to Drancy and thereafter to the death camps. The German soldiers of the Brehmer Division had, it seems, received the order in the spring of 1944 to kill on the spot all male Jews and to deport only women and children. Might this be one of the clues to the murder of Chaim, also known as Jem?

But the surprise for me is elsewhere on the memorial: right at the top of the list, placed like a pebble washed up on a beach, the

spelling somewhat speculative, doubtless as a result of hasty transcription from a handwritten document, with a strange hyphenated
given name: Rozen Chaine-Mendel.

What is he doing here, our hairdresser/musician? His presence
at the head of the list is indeed rather surprising: he did not live
in Lacelle and he died within the boundaries of the neighbouring
commune. Why and when was it agreed to place his name on this
little memorial? The explanation is probably to be found in the
fact that the two communes – Lacelle and L'Église-aux-Bois – like
many others, have been forced to merge in recent years following
an intercommunal agreement. Who would have thought that Jem,
the violinist hailing from Poland and Belgium, would one day, so
long after his death, be mixed up in the reform of French rural
administration?

A little after All Saints' Day, I push open the door of the
mairie and go in. Three or four men are chatting about the clear
cold nights we are having and the onset of the hoar frosts, about
the mushrooms that no longer grow under the Douglas pines,
about the leaves that have not yet fallen and about the next match
to be played by the French rugby team on tour in the southern
hemisphere. An open window lets the last rays of the afternoon
sun reach the middle of the room. My questions about events
occurring during the last war provoke not so much discomfort
as polite surprise. They respond evasively but with the best will
in the world. All that happened so long ago. They have no personal memory of the events, a few echoes might have come to
them from some parents, others never spoke of the past. They
suggest I would be better off consulting the former town clerk,
now retired. He was there throughout the war. 'He knows a lot
of things.' But they warn me that 'it will all depend on how you
approach him…'

I find out that the current memorial was put up after some
protests – emanating in part from people who did not even live in

the commune – because the old memorial listed the names of the adults killed by the Germans on 4 April, but not those of the Jewish children deported the same day. This was at the beginning of the 1990s. The protests were followed by a good deal of controversy during which old misgivings, half-forgotten suspicions and resentments came to the surface again. For many inhabitants, things are still not entirely clear. 'How did it come about that these children were arrested? Were they selected on the basis of the teachers' registers? Were they arrested in the actual school grounds? No one is certain about any of this.' The town clerk, at my request, leafs through the minutes of the council's discussions to trace back the decision to replace the memorial at the beginning of the 1990s, or at least the debates that accompanied the establishment of the new memorial. No record of either.

Today the younger inhabitants talk about those days with a certain detachment. It was all so long ago. There is no one left to get angry, to contradict, to remain silent. I ask if I can see the former plaque which has certainly not been destroyed. I would like to see if the name of Jem/Chaim was originally there or if it has been added only on this occasion. Someone gets keys, doors are opened. 'I know I have seen that plaque somewhere, not so long ago...' But no one can put their hand on it. Once again, the past slips away from me. I promise myself that one day I will come back and continue the search.

The majority of the last living witnesses cannot provide any information because, in all good faith (for the most part), they remember nothing, or almost nothing. Because Alzheimer's disease is a formidable rival, continually digging its burrows. Because my informants either never knew or forgot immediately. Much time, luck and determination are needed to discover the irrefutable evidence that can counter such a weight of forgetfulness and indifference.

It was a curious schoolteacher on secondment to the school in Lacelle who, at the beginning of the 1990s, found in the back of a cupboard the old class register kept by one of his distant predecessors. In the notebook covered with the dust of 1944, the then schoolteacher had written carefully in purple ink, opposite the names of the six pupils, repeated six times: 'taken by the German police on 4 April 1944, burned in Aus.'

So it did happen. No one could doubt it any longer. Some did doubt, however, to the extent of hiding for a time the awkward registers. A few hard heads continue to deny, exclaiming, 'Whatever is this story you are telling?' You should have questioned some of the people who are now dead, I am frequently told, especially those who have recently died for, it seems, those are the people who knew everything. The absence of any memory of these events can only be explained by the premature death of the witnesses who would have ensured it lasted forever (the most precious, the most irreplaceable is always the one who has most recently passed on). And so, in a school in Corrèze, six children whose parents had lived in the town for months, who walked along the high street every day, their satchels on their backs, simply disappeared forever on a fine spring morning, taken by their oppressors in a truck headed for an unknown destination.

Two days later, Jem/Chaim also went through Lacelle, driven in a similar military truck, seated between two soldiers. But he did not get as far as Limoges. Nor Drancy, nor Auschwitz. His journey stopped short, between two trees, a little further along on the edge of the main road. He is lying in a neighbouring cemetery. He never left the country, his body was not consumed in smoke. His name, which can be found today at the very top of the memorial, does not figure on the fading lists kept by the accountants of the deportation. In his death, he has the good fortune, unlike the millions of other victims of the Shoah, to possess a grave, a little bit of ground that belongs to him.

The Future of the Past

Fort de Charenton, Tulle, Paris, Limoges, 2003

THERE IS SOMETHING REASSURING ABOUT THE ROOMS in which archives are kept. Everything looks so neat and orderly. In the police archives, stored at the Fort de Charenton in the suburbs of Paris, the files have recently been renewed, the cloth covered cardboard folders have no accumulated layers of dust, the straps around the bundles have been tightly knotted by vigorous young police archivists who disdain the slapdash habits of bored clerks. Several bundles have never been opened and strong hands are needed to untie the straps. In the well-lit reading room, whose windows overlook beautiful lawns where, from time to time, troops must parade, everything is classified, labelled, calm. It feels uncanny nevertheless to be entering for the first time into an unexplored and unpredictable universe. As the popular saying has it, one never knows what tomorrow will bring. For me now, it is as if the events of the past have not already taken place and I do not know what the past will bring. To immerse oneself in the archives is to give the past a future all over again. At the very least, it is to give the past a chance, to refuse to accept uncritically the official sequence of events which works to shape and delimit the story for all time. It means refusing to accept as Holy Writ the familiar chain of cause and effect. From the moment the helpful police clerk in charge of the reading room shows you how to fill in the first order form to obtain the first file for your next visit – 'it will be brought in two days' time by shuttle from Versailles' – the die is cast: the past is surging into the present. Police records are particularly valuable in resurrecting the minutiae of daily life at the local level. I cannot wait to open the files that, from as early as 1945, document inquiries carried out in the heat of the moment into the atrocities committed by the German army in the months preceding and immediately following the Liberation.

In the country, where departmental records are now stored in modern office buildings that, in Tulle and Limoges, dominate the surrounding townscape, there is the same calm and peaceful atmosphere. The reading rooms are, however, often extremely crowded, filled to capacity with retirees busily consulting the archives of parish and *mairie* in order to research their family history. It is advisable to get there early in order to find a good seat and to have the documents brought promptly. Records dealing with the last war are classified under 'W'. I am reassured to discover that showing an interest in the 'W' category brings one to the attention of the curators, all of whom are pleasant and efficient, but who are very alert to the use that might be made of these still highly sensitive documents, made accessible only recently to the general public.

No readers are more engrossed in their work than those in the reading rooms of the public records offices. For hours on end the only sound to be heard is the soft rustling of pages being turned. Totally absorbed in their quests, these thesis writers and genealogy buffs, researchers, collectors and amateurs of all sorts, hardly raise their heads, they pore over documents, make notes and assess the work that remains to be done; they are insatiable and, above all, always eager to open up the next bundle of documents, the one they have just ordered. They are like gamblers: it is the next folder that might contain the jackpot, the information they have almost given up hope of finding. The silence is thus occasionally broken by little sounds, a brief laugh, a gasp of amazement or indignation at a striking discovery. These little gestures and spontaneous sounds are immediately repressed, stifled, but they attract the attention of those sitting nearest, provoking in them barely perceptible responses of irritation, empathy or envy. Silence quickly resumes its dominance, however, as there is nothing more absorbing than the search for truths that are forever beyond one's grasp. Newly discovered facts constantly undermine previous certainties.

Surprisingly, there is no such contemplative silence in the reading room at the Contemporary Jewish Documentation Centre in Paris. In the premises where it used to be housed, at the far end of a paved courtyard in the Marais, as in the new building close by where it has recently moved, protected by security guards and surveillance cameras, it is a unique place dedicated to the preservation of knowledge concerning the Shoah. The millions of victims of Nazi racism are gathered there *post mortem*. Committed young archivists are on duty, eager to advise Jewish visitors from around the world on how best to conduct their searches, half a century after the event, for any new information concerning the existence on earth or the death of members of their close and extended families. People consult their laptops, boot up the microfilm readers, reopen the old typed and sometimes handwritten index cards, they ask questions, and above all they listen to the elderly ladies who recount their own experiences in accents from every country in Europe. In the old building, this used to create a strange kind of animated atmosphere, particularly on the days when, at the other end of the windowless room in the Rue de Turenne, a group of old people, speaking both French and Yiddish, would laugh and joke as they evoked their memories of the 'world of yesterday'. In the reading room of the ultra modern new premises of the Memorial, sunlight shines in through the Stars of David carved into the concrete. The grey book lying on the librarian's counter, Serge Klarsfeld's encyclopaedic listing of the names of all those deported in the convoys, is still the same volume, worn and tattered now from so much handling. But one gets the strong impression nevertheless that in this place history is gradually taking over from memory.

At certain moments during the course of my investigation, I have felt that the archives were bringing me close to discovering a fragment of the truth. The bundles of discoloured paper and faded Manila folders consulted in many different archival collections have divulged secrets, some little and some big. Handwritten in ink or pencil, often typed on machines with worn out ribbons, some-times held together by vicious, rusty pins, they have revealed facts one could not have suspected, all the while concealing others one despairs of ever flushing out. This concealment is sometimes due simply to bad luck or carelessness, sometimes to deliberate acts. So, for instance, the records of the Bugeat brigade of the gendarmerie, meticulously kept up to this point, suddenly cease on 17 February 1944. They then resume, with no comment or explanation, at the beginning of the summer. The pages covering the period of the major actions carried out by the Resistance, the events of the 'week of bloodshed', of the Liberation and the reprisals against collaborators that followed have all disappeared. They were not ripped out in haste but very deliberately and neatly cut out.

I will discover subsequently that this is not an isolated case but that the records of many other brigades of the gendarmerie in the region have been similarly expurgated. What had to be hidden? When was it decided that there should be a systematic censorship of the months preceding the Liberation? Was it immediately after the defeat of the Germans or later? Who took the initiative? It is difficult to imagine that, in such a disciplined and hierarchical organisation, the decision to erase the past would have been taken anywhere other than at the highest military and political levels.

This gap in the principal record does not erase what preceded it: the police archives contain much valuable material concerning the first three years of the war, providing information about what really happened. They give details about the first 'relocation operations' carried out in the summer of 1942 in the southern zone under the authority of the chief constable of the Vichy police, René Bousquet. They report, notably, that on 26 August near the village of Barsanges, gendarmes from outside the area arrested a score of Jews who had been conscripted alongside Spanish refugee workers in the GTE responsible for digging peat. All of those arrested disappeared at dawn and were never heard from again. Daily reports from the gendarmerie indicate that it was at this time that the local constabulary undertook the first 'sweep' to arrest all foreign Jews, fortunately with little success. (The term 'sweep' seems to emerge spontaneously in reports and official records of the time: law enforcers and bureaucrats all use it to designate these night-time round-ups.) Others then followed, notably at the beginning of 1943.

Numerous reports indicate in minute detail how the gendarmes knocked on doors long after night had fallen and then dispatched their prey while the rest of the town slept. Some policemen in certain brigades (ashamed perhaps?), having taken it upon themselves to wear plain clothes for these operations, were promptly brought to heel by written orders from superior officers: full uniform must be worn when carrying out the government's dirty work. The time of the operation is always given with meticulous accuracy: between three and six o'clock in the morning. In this way, the spectacle of the arrests was hidden from the bulk of the population. Neighbours, on waking in the morning, discover only that the shutters on the house opposite remain closed that day. The house will not remain empty for long, such is the shortage of accommodation. And of course there will always be someone who will offer to clean up the house, to pack up and store in his own house the pathetic belongings abandoned by the fugitives and deportees...

Still hoping to find or establish a full list of victims of all the 'sweeps' in the canton, I must be satisfied in the meantime with picking up a name or two from the margins of the archives, sometimes simply handwritten pages torn from a child's exercise book. Henri Monheit, arrested 20 February 1943 in Tarnac, was taken to the relocation camp at Ségur-le-Château. Ruben Wohl, Abraham Halgzjait, Osias Gutwein, all three Jews originally from Poland, were arrested in Pérols a few days later. The gendarmes, who carry out their work in a thoroughly professional and conscientious manner and cannot be deflected, note for the benefit of those who will carry out a 'screening' (another new word to designate the first stage of the selection process for those to be sent to forced labour and to death camps) that Ruben Wohl is married, that his wife has already been deported and that he has a sixteen-year-old daughter. Similarly, they report that Abraham Halgzait' is also married, that he has a nineteen-month-old baby daughter, that he has a disabled hand and is therefore capable only of 'light work', that Osias Gutwein, aged sixty-four, is married and childless, that he is a 'minister of religion: rabbi' (opposite his name, however, scribbled in pencil, a single word: qualified). These annotations suggest that some gendarmes try not to make things worse for those they are arresting, are even hinting discreetly at possible grounds for defence. Those four men are nevertheless sent to Auschwitz in the first days of March 1943, in convoys 50, 51, or later in convoy 62.

The reports of the gendarmerie never state that the Resistance has intervened to block the arrests of Jews, but they do indicate that, tipped off in time by the inhabitants who lodge and protect them, many of the designated victims manage to escape before the sweeps and disappear into the countryside. The gendarmes engage in exhaustive enquiries to track the comings and goings of this or that individual, who might well alternate periods in hiding with returns to the village. They collect multiple fragments of information but along the way may provide tip-offs that save lives. They establish endless lists of names, publish them and then establish new lists. They are obliged to make countless reports to the higher echelons of their own hierarchy, and to the bureaucrats who run the administration of the department, all of whom pounce with delight on these infamous lists. The lists have not been established just to gather dust in bottom drawers. And the more the situation deteriorates for the occupying forces, the more these drawers are opened up. Just before the 'week of bloodshed', all the prefects received an unequivocal telegram from the headquarters of the national police in Vichy: 'Authorisation hereby granted to provide accredited German officials lists of French and foreign Jews should they request same.'

As numbers in the brigade have not been increased, the gendarmes of Bugeat are overwhelmed by the work. Their results are far from the most brilliant in the department! Their officers are worried, which can be seen now as a mark in favour of the gendarmes. It must be added that in July 1943 each member of the brigade received by post a letter addressed to him by name containing a warning from the Resistance which must have made many of them think twice: 'You are in a tricky situation. Your job requires that you hunt us down. Your conscience tells you to support us.' The import of this anonymous communication must have been in the minds of officers throughout the months until the beginning of the next summer, right up until the day when the Resistance took over the whole of the gendarmerie without a shot being fired. In the immaculately tidy reading room at the Fort de Charenton,

I look up for a moment from the yellowing bundles of papers. I watch the helpful young officers busily coming and going in the room and wonder if they have any idea what is sleeping in these cardboard boxes full of old papers they carry about all day long.

In connection with lists, an impressive document suddenly emerges from the mass of archival material: a census of foreigners living in the canton on 30 July 1943, carried out by the local brigade of the gendarmerie. Two large format pages that open facing each other and look as though they could have formed part of the double-entry bookkeeping in a commercial enterprise, names carefully typed in columns, practically no typographical errors or crossings out. Surnames and given names, followed by the date and place of birth, nationality and the commune of current residence. There are nearly 150 names of foreigners who have come from all over Europe and the Mediterranean, the vast majority being Spanish republicans and Jews. A very neat job indeed, in spite of some quaint guesswork (a woman born in Constantinople has been given the nationality 'Constantine'!).[2]

This synoptic table, holiday homework for the gendarmes over the summer of 1943, on which they expended so much effort, provides an insight into the cosmopolitan make-up of the Plateau during the years of the war, but it says nothing about the numbers of Jews who disappeared as a result of the various 'sweeps' carried out in the canton. To write history is to fill in blanks. In our local history, a large number of blanks remain. Notably, in connection with these 'sweeps' that were carried out with the utmost circumspection right up until the Liberation. How many 'sweeps' were there? What is known is that they were of various types: some were vast, centrally planned at the national or regional level, and others seem to have been what might be called local initiatives. The brutality of these actions, the separations, social isolation and fear for the future they provoked meant that families lived their lives in utter terror and confusion. There is no instrument that can measure the nature of despair, all we have are the scattered fragments that have somehow ended up in the archives, such as this telegram, a cry from the heart addressed to the prefect of Corrèze, sent from the post office in Tarnac on 27 February 1943 at 10.40 a.m.: 'HUSBAND TAKEN BEG YOU DO ALL POSSIBLE FOR RELEASE: MADAME DE HAAF.' The telegram with its capital letters pasted onto blue paper certainly reached its destination, it was not thrown into the wastepaper basket. It was filed by the meticulous clerks working at the prefecture. And there it is still today, adrift in the middle of a thick folder. It speaks only of the utter desolation of this woman.

The files have banal titles: 'Sent to Occupied Zone', 'Transferred within Occupied Zone'. Never any further afield. Thinking of the mindset of the people who created these files, I wonder if it is possible tell how much was due to ignorance, blindness, habit, disbelief, how much to cowardice or professionalism. It requires an effort to decode the repressive administrative jargon in order to appreciate the way it functions to camouflage disturbing realities: for example, French bureaucrats never speak of the 'German troops' who are devastating the Plateau, but only of 'campaign troops'.

Anyone delving at all deeply into the archives of the period will quickly get used to the doublespeak employed by the Vichy regime and will also discover a surprising number of local sources of written material. In sub-prefectures, prefectures and ministerial offices, not to mention in the various military authorities and the French and German police forces, reports, circulars and memoranda continued to accumulate until the final day of defeat for some, victory for others, and sometimes continuing beyond that day as though nothing out of the ordinary had happened. It is of course well known that the most desirable quality of an administrative department – as of a head of protocol – is to remain unflappable whatever the circumstances. In some archival collections, however, it is not uncommon to find a sudden disarray in the filing that bears witness to the upheaval going on outside the offices. For example, at the end of spring 1944, at the prefecture in Limoges, the reports from all the gendarmeries in the Dordogne are for several weeks mixed up with those coming from Haute-Vienne and Corrèze, and personal requests addressed to the prefect are filed together with memoranda from the Vichy government. Not total chaos, just a slight and very temporary muddle caused by the tempest raging in the country. Taking advantage of the lucky breaks created by these moments when administrative oversight is briefly relaxed, one may discover a report from a gendarme or an inspector that has been misfiled and turned up in a folder where it had no business to be, thus providing a detail that has been either voluntarily or involuntarily suppressed.

In the entrance hall to the departmental archives of Haute-Vienne, in Limoges, I linger for a moment to look at an exhibition devoted to the 1914 war, as it was lived in the Limousin. I discover that patriotic fervour in the Great War was by no means as intense or as unanimous as has been claimed for so long. Documents dating from the period, unearthed by scrupulous archivists, completely subvert the received wisdom. Negative attitudes – rebellious, free-thinking, anarcho-syndicalist, pacifist – had caused such upheavals among the working class in Limoges and Saint-Junien that police were deployed in force in 1917 to control a crowd of angry women who were blocking the departure of a train taking men who had been on leave back to the front. They were determined to protect their sons, their husbands, their lovers; they were refusing to let any more go and die for the fatherland. I read the notes of the police inspector and I look at the old photographs that show a whole community expressing its anger. This is a long way from the flower bedecked rifles that dominate the memories of my parents' generation. I had almost forgotten that I was not here for this, but to attempt to uncover new evidence about the life and the death of victims of the next war to afflict the Limousin high country.

In public records offices, as long as you can avoid getting lost in the labyrinth of the filing system and are able to work through large masses of papers that might well have been filed under peripheral headings, then you will nearly always eventually find what you are looking for. Or you will find something you were not looking for but which throws light on it. It is a question of time. I leaf through files quickly, too quickly, I strain my eyes attempting to decipher notes written by hand or typed onto flimsy paper which is unable to retain the typewriter ink in use at the time, technology that is both modern and already out of date. But my reward comes at last – after the pain, the gain.

Here it is in front of me, the official document that I was not able to find when I first began to search in the departmental archives in Tulle! Dated 18 April 1944, catalogued now under call number ADHV 185 W3/31, it was sent from the office of the prefect of Corrèze.[3] The note is addressed to the regional prefect in Limoges and it contains a summary account of events, lists the names, correctly spelled, of the victims of 6 April, all the victims, 'the blokes from L'Echameil' and the Jews, including Chaim. The arrest of a number of children is finally acknowledged by the administrative authorities. Their names are not given, as though they are not important enough for that, but the relationship of four of them to a certain Marie Kleinberg is noted: 'The two children of Mme Kleinberg, aged respectively 11 and 9 years, her two nieces aged 15 and 5 years who were living with her were taken as well as the son of Mme Tencer, aged 3 years.' Date of birth and nationality are listed opposite the name of each adult. All the adults are of Polish nationality, except Lucie Fribourg, the only one to have French nationality. Opposite each name, the precision striking me each time with shock and disbelief: 'Race Jew'.

I know where to find the names of the children. The meticulous officers at the camp in Drancy, I am sure, will not have let them leave in a convoy headed for Auschwitz without having first made careful note of their names, places and dates of birth. In order to be certain that each one of them was accounted for, that each should figure on the only list that really meant anything: the list of victims of the final solution. Before entering the gas chambers, one's identity had to be confirmed.

Once again, the research carried out by Serge Klarsfeld reveals its incomparable value. In Room J of the National Library of France, surrounded by a crowd of students preparing for mid-term examinations, I have come to consult his list of Jews arrested in France. It is always to his work that I turn to seek confirmation for what was otherwise only intuition and hypothesis. Missing details are often to be found there, buried in the endless, sombre lists, accompanied by sparse commentaries: Marie Kleinberg, née Izbicka, was raising her two daughters, Anna and Rosa (both born in Metz), and her two nieces, Anna and Jeanne Izbicka (born in Poland, probably refugees in Lorraine at the beginning of the war). So these children I have been looking for ever since I first read the footnote in *The Maquis of the Corrèze* were members of the same family. Lying on the page, among so many tens of thousands of others, their given names bring irrefutable proof of the passage on this earth of four children. To these four must be added Mme Tencer's little boy, who was born in Paris at the beginning of the war and whose name was Serge.[4]

Around me, the young people hardly look up from their notepads and laptops. They are so used to the comfort that surrounds them, to the well-regulated temperature of the reading rooms, the long tables of dark wood, the neat rows of ergonomically designed chairs, and the light reflected peacefully in the tall windows overlooking the enclosed garden. How is it possible, in this place, to evoke the reality of the cold, the humiliation, to experience the separation, fear, cruelty and barbarity? This evening, librarians will pick up the volume by Serge Klarsfeld and the other books dealing with the deportations I have been consulting and they will put them back on the shelves reserved for French history. We are fortunate indeed that nothing occurs to disturb the good order and the studious calm of our libraries.

Jewish Easter

Haute-Corrèze, 6 April 1944

WRITTEN ARCHIVES CAN REINFORCE PERSONAL TES-
timonies or undermine them, and so one must go constantly from one to the other. Consulting the archives produces a
rather different picture of the events of 6 April. It is still the same
Holy Thursday, and the same soldiers, hunting Resistance fighters,
occupy the town early that morning and arrest and kill four hostages, residents of the hamlet of L'Echameil. However, alongside
these events, in the same places and at the same moments, there
are other acts of violence occurring off screen, there are other
characters, other lives affected.

Right at the centre of town, the barber's shop. In the country it
is not uncommon for men to come to get their hair cut soon after
daybreak, so Jem comes to work early, as on other days. Just
before the German troops surround the town. But the rumbling of
the armoured vehicles, the heavy wheezing of the trucks and the
commotion of the soldiers going up and down the Rue Nationale

throw him into a state of terror. He has only one idea in his head: to warn Malka, his wife, to protect his family, his daughters, his brother. Is the only mission of this detachment of soldiers that has arrived so unexpectedly to hunt down Resistance fighters and to try to dismantle their camps? As an active member of the Resistance, his employer is trying not to give in to panic. Might he have been betrayed, might the door of the barber's salon be about to be thrown open with a crash? His mind races: will he manage to keep quiet under torture, will he still be alive this evening? Behind the thin partition wall that separates the shop from the living quarters, he can hear his wife getting breakfast ready for the children. There is no conversation in the salon. The clicking of the scissors is louder than the sound of the first customers scraping their clogs.

The barber is hardly older than Jem, but he is already a mature man. The experience of political activism acquired before the war helps him to keep his fear under control. He wants to give Jem some of his hard-won self-discipline. He reasons with him. He tries to dissuade him from going out. He advises him to chat with customers, to sweep up, to pretend to sweep up, to wait until lunchtime or perhaps until nightfall. No long arguments, a few short phrases, hints. But Jem cannot be persuaded. He is overcome by his anxiety. He is thinking about his little girls, Shifra and Hanna, whom he had rushed to bring back only a few weeks earlier from the children's home where they were no longer safe. In the house up the hill, they have already begun to play, to squabble. Malka is looking after them while also preparing the layette for the new baby: she is due to give birth in a few weeks. Far away from all the commotion, she is probably still unaware there is anything wrong.

He thinks about his brother Jacob, whom he has got into the habit of calling Jacques like everyone else does: it seems like another world when he remembers that before the war Jacques was a tap dancer, a singer, entertainer and incorrigible day-dreamer. He must also be at work this morning, standing at his workbench a few hundred metres away. Four members of his family, soon to be five, all closely related to him, come from so far away, from Poland, a country that no one here has any idea about, that even he has difficulty picturing, after so many flights, at last gathered all together in this little town in the Limousin, spared, almost safe, and yet suddenly in dire peril. The roots of his family go back a long way, they have lived for generations in a town called Girardof or Żyrardów, near Warsaw, a town named after a French engineer named Philippe de Girard, who settled there at the beginning of the nineteenth century and contributed to its development by inventing revolutionary new techniques for the local textile industry. Before that, the town was called Mszczonów. That is where he was born in 1910. And it is from there that, before him, the Wagners and the Rozents, all artists and entertainers, flocked into Byelorussia, and particularly into Belgium. He thinks of his father, Ben Zion, playwright, actor, Yiddish and polyglot journalist, a major figure in the theatre world of Antwerp, who died when he himself was still a teen-ager. He thinks most particularly of his mother, a well-known actress, whom he tried to protect right up until the end, until the day she was arrested in Sète, and deported. That was barely two years ago. He does not dare think about all the others who stayed in Poland, family members he hardly knows, of whom he has heard nothing.

The noose is tightening. He knows that the Jewish families who have sought refuge on the Plateau – whether they are French or foreign – have been placed under house arrest, their names are on files kept by the *mairie*, the gendarmerie, the prefecture, the man-agement of the Foreign Workers' Brigade, the police in Limoges and in Tulle, because there are lists everywhere. The Gestapo and the Militia,* just to speak the words freezes the blood, are keeping them under surveillance from afar and they, too, keep lists, as do the German soldiers. He had to go underground for several weeks at the end of last year, had to vanish into the wilds in order to escape the deportation he suspected would have resulted from the official summons he had decided to ignore.

At this time everyone feels under threat, but for some the threat is far more real than for others. Among the most in danger are, of course, the fighters in the maquis. Emboldened by the situation on all the fronts of the war and by the coming invasion of France by Allied forces, they have been increasing the frequency of spectacular armed attacks, particularly in this region. They are the primary objective of the German soldiers. But surely it would be miraculous if Jews, and more especially foreign Jews, were not also to be targeted in this punitive raid by the Germans. The troops hunting down Resistance units in this region where the Communist Party was well entrenched before the war do not bother with minor details: everyone is swept up into the same bag, dubbed Judeo-Bolshevik. Jem has never heard of General Lammerding, commander of Das Reich Division, stationed in the South-West, who frequently says 'find the partisan and you will find the Jew,' but he has no illusions about the intentions of the Nazi regime, henceforth on the defensive, nor of the French authorities that have been collaborating with it. He has not forgotten that gendarmes confiscated the identity papers of all the Jewish refugees as soon as they arrived on the special train that brought them from the south of France. None of these people, in particular the members of his own family, can any longer consider themselves to be citizens like any other, they are no longer free agents. Have they not already been condemned?

---

* The Militia (Milice Française) was a greatly feared paramilitary force, established by the Vichy regime in 1943 to assist the Germans in fighting the Resistance and in rounding up Jews for deportation. [Note from the translator]

Jem does not think of himself as a hero. He wants to save the people who are nearest and dearest to him. The reiterated advice of the barber does not persuade him. It is not Jem who makes the decision: it is his anguish and the strength of his emotion that confront the danger, that place his hand on the door handle. In order to avoid the high street, which can be crossed in a few strides, he probably decides to slip along the lane that runs parallel to the road, along the track of the ancient '*turgotière*'.* But there is no way he can avoid going across the square, passing by the war memorial (it was located there at that time), walking openly, forcing himself to walk at a normal pace, hiding his clenched fists in his pockets, touching the comb and the scissors that he had not even thought to put down. He will not get any further. Soldiers on duty stop him in front of the Hôtel de Paris, because he is young, because all the men of his age are under suspicion of being in the Resistance. They discover that he is a Jew, his name is on their lists. How do they find out that he has participated in the clandestine dances held in the neighbourhood – that is to say that he must be in touch with the maquis? Have they been tipped off? Jem's arrest puts in danger part of the local organisation of the Resistance. Will he crack? The barber and several of those close to him now have even more to fear.

At this stage, it must be admitted, the written archives have nothing to say, and witness statements are rare and contradictory. It is probable that the SS, who run these kinds of punitive expeditions, are in a hurry, they have not got time to compare data, check files or undertake orthodox questioning. They doubtless prefer rough and ready methods. As a putative organiser of clandestine dances, suspected of knowing the whereabouts of the Resistance camps, he will be subjected to a ruthless interrogation. His brother

---

* A remnant of the network of roads established in the eighteenth century by Baron Turgot while he was intendant of Limoges before becoming Louis XIV's minister of finance.

Jacob later confided to those close to him that his brother was brutally tortured. He is commanded over and over again to tell them where the 'terrorists' are hiding. Savagely beaten, facing the machine guns, staring down the black hole of a rifle barrel, he plays for time, promises to speak to the 'Kommandantur'. Hence the decision to transport him immediately to Limoges and hand him over to the Gestapo.

In the town, while the ordinary soldiers are busy setting up their quarters, the little troop of SS continues its 'work'. They are there not only to catch draft dodgers and Resistance fighters, but also to arrest Jews. Not only foreign Jews, as was the case for a long time: now it is all Jews, even women and children, even those with French nationality. But how, in the street, can one recognise who is a Jew and who is not? In earlier round-ups, it has happened that locals from the region have been arrested by mistake. In this part of the country, Jews do not wear the yellow star. It is true that there are numerous lists and soldiers in all armies of occupation are crazy about lists. But lists are not enough. The soldiers have to go and search for the Jews where they are hiding. In order to ferret them out, the German soldiers need local guides.

For several months now, apart from the nights when rumours have spread about an imminent sweep, the Jews have been hiding relatively little. Even though warnings passed on by neighbours have saved them in the past, many have grown tired of having to 'hole up' yet again. Besides this, many now feel that they are no longer in any real danger. In spite of the fact that the Germans have now occupied the southern zone, Jews bearing French nationality in particular do not dream that they are 'deportable'. They think they are safe because they are more than sixty years old, because they have wives and children who are also French, because the men have served in the French army, because they are in poor health, or simply because they have tried to be model citizens, taking care to obey all the ever proliferating and oppressive regulations imposed on them by the Vichy regime. Surely people who obey the law must be protected, mustn't they? These are all convincing arguments, aren't they?

Towards the middle of the morning, some German soldiers are selected and told to go and arrest Jews. But which Jews? Essentially those who are working closest to the centre of town. The *garde-champêtre** serves as guide. The man whose normal job consists of walking around the town beating a drum and making public announcements, is now knocking on doors, explaining to householders and to tenants just what is wanted by the soldier who has accompanied him. Everything happens very peacefully, as though nothing out of the ordinary is happening. Lucie Fribourg and Clara Uhlmann, who are renting accommodation in neighbouring houses and often go on long walks together, who have become friends, are relieved to be together at this moment. The two elderly ladies, who have been given just enough time to throw a coat around their shoulders, are seen by very few people as they walk through the town. The streets are virtually deserted.

The members of the Kleinberg family, who came from Lorraine as part of the mass exodus of 1940 and have been living since the beginning of the war in a house at the top of the Rue Nationale, make a great catch. Five in one go. It is well known that Marie Kleinberg has been bringing up her two daughters and her two nieces. The youngest of the children is only six years old and the eldest nearly sixteen. Pointing to one of the girls – afflicted with a disability, so I am told – a neighbour dares to speak up:

---

*   The *garde-champêtre* is a lowly public official employed by the commune in rural areas of France, part forest ranger and part police officer. The French term is used as there is no equivalent post in rural administration elsewhere. [Note from the translator]

'Surely you are not going to take that one too...' But it is in vain. Everyone does what they are told and the little group sets off in silence.

Carola Hoch, for her part, leaves the apartment she has been renting as soon as she receives a hint of the danger. She is also a native of Lorraine and arrived in Bugeat nearly three years ago. She knows a lot of people and knows where to seek assistance. Carrying a suitcase, she hid for a while in the woodpile belonging to a neighbour, then she ran a little further to seek refuge in the house of the nurse who gives her an injection every morning. When the local official and the German soldier knock at her door, her landlady tells them that her tenant is out and that she does not know where she has gone. But the neighbour's little son is playing on the pavement and he knows the *garde-champêtre* very well: his cap and the sort of uniform he wears make him an important figure in the child's eyes. The child knows exactly where Mme Hoch is, he has just seen her, he wants to be helpful: he saw her go to the nurse's house. His little finger points the way.

This is not a vicious pogrom, it is a series of non-violent arrests, more like a simple exercise of administrative identity checks. The women and children gather on the square, opposite the church and the *mairie*. The adults, who know each other by sight, make nervous little gestures of recognition.

That morning, at exactly the same time, on the other side of France, police from the Gestapo led by Klaus Barbie collect forty-four Jewish children and ransack the house where their parents and teachers had hidden them and believed them to be in safety. The children of Bugeat are like the children of Izieu: at this precise moment they are unaware of what is in store for them but their terror can be seen in their eyes.

The unusual noises and the silence have alerted all the Jewish families living in different parts of the town, striking terror into their hearts. Regardless of the sentries posted around the exit roads, some doubtless seek refuge in the nearby forest. Others lie trembling in their normal hiding places. Has Jem's wife, Malka, witnessed the arrest of the Kleinberg family from the house opposite, watching from behind the curtains of her front room and clasping her two little daughters in her arms? When does she learn that Jem has been arrested?

Towards midday, Jem is brought to the square where the Jewish women and children have been gathered together with Mme Vacher, who saw her husband taken along with the other hostages but does not yet know that he has already been killed. All are pushed onto the platform of an open truck, crowded together at the far end while the soldiers sit along the sides, leaning against the tailboard. The truck does a U-turn in order to take the road for Limoges.

Two hours later, a good ten kilometres from there, Jem's body is found by the farmer who lives at the property called L'Omelette that overlooks the main road. He sees right away that the dead man is not anyone he knows. His clothes suggest a town dweller, he is wearing a navy blue suit and tan shoes. In the jacket pocket is nothing but a comb and a pair of barber's scissors.

The spot where Jem was murdered is not just anywhere. At virtually the same place, just after the series of hairpin bends on the tree lined road overhanging the steep descent to the river, close to the railway viaduct, on 28 March, only a few days earlier, the three Citroën front-wheel drives belonging to the Armistice Commission in Limoges, made up of French and German officers, were ambushed by a group of Resistance fighters led by Guingouin, who was beginning at that time to be known as the prefect of the Resistance. The German officers were shot dead without any form of trial. How can one think that this event did not affect General Brehmer's decision to send one of his diabolical units, based in the Dordogne, into this remote corner of the Haute-Corrèze? Murdered at the exact spot where blood had already been spilled, Jem can be seen also as a victim of the primitive law of an eye for an eye.

The scene probably went something like this: the truck draws up on the side of the road. The German soldiers force Jem to get out, just him, they press the machine gun against his back once again, demand once again that he divulge the whereabouts of the Resistance fighters who kill German officers and organise clandestine dances, that he give them the names of these terrorists. Confronted with his determined silence, the shot rings out. The truck drives off with its load of petrified women and children, leaving behind a motionless body, lying beside a ditch. 'Height one metre sixty-five, hair curly dark brown' as the death certificate will state. Jem was killed because he was Jewish but also because he refused to speak.

The little SS detachment with its lieutenant leaves Bugeat in the middle of the afternoon. They take the road towards Tarnac in order to commit more crimes, as is now known. The corpses of the four hostages from L'Echameil lie abandoned near the birch wood. The town is no longer sealed off but the population remains behind closed doors.

Jacques, the brother of Jem, waits until evening before leaving his workshop. In order to look unobtrusive, he takes the hand of a little child he knows who often plays at that spot and they walk together along the edge of the fields for a while, chatting about this and that, as though they were part of the same family. Then Jacques takes to his heels until he gets to the woods high up beyond the town, towards Le Massoutre, where he can hide.

Opposite the Kleinbergs' empty house, the Rozents' house is also empty. Malka has fled with her two children. Perhaps she has managed to join her brother-in-law and is hiding with him for this first night. From now on she must face the dangers on her own: she must get the children to a place of safety, find somewhere to live, to prepare for the birth of her baby who will now have no father. One daughter in her arms, the other clinging tightly to her skirt, she takes to the road. Seeking refuge in Tulle, she has no idea that she is walking straight into another death trap: in two months' time the prefecture of Corrèze will be occupied and ransacked by the Das Reich Division. Flee and flee again.

Forty-eight hours later in Limoges, at the synagogue on the Rue Cruveilhier, Rabbi Abraham Deutsch tells the small congregation gathered for the sabbath service, 'At the present time, Israel has indeed become the lamb of God, slaughtered by the nations.' This year, according to the Church calendar, the Jewish Easter will fall on the same day as the Christian. But how in these conditions will it be possible to celebrate Passover?

At the end of April, the prefect of the Corrèze, Pierre Trouillé, will return to the 'week of bloodshed' in the monthly report he regularly sends to the Vichy government. Impassive servant of the state, he will write: 'The round-up of foreigners by German and French authorities was particularly well received by the inhabitants of Corrèze who object to this category of foreigner.'

A Beautiful Summer

Haute-Corrèze, 13–14 July 2004

T HE TOURISTS ARE BEGINNING TO ARRIVE, SHUTTERS are being thrown open in the most isolated houses. In the shops and at the campsite, conversations turn sooner or later to the weather forecasts: everybody is wondering if the farmers will be able to harvest the hay in time, given the uncertain start to the season and whether there will be a repeat of last year's heatwave. Many express doubts about that but warnings abound: 'You can't trust the weather, last year the heatwave started much later, towards the end of July.'

The other subject of conversation is the Tour de France. This year the race will pass through the neighbouring canton. Even if this year they are going around the base of the Monédières, the cyclists are going to have to scale the foothills and that means a long uphill climb on a road with hairpin bends, it's going to be a magnificent spectacle, not to be missed. There is competition for the best places on the slopes from which to watch the race and its procession of support vehicles, the most sought after spots are shaded by a beech tree and overlook one of the sharp bends. At the bakery and the delicatessen, the butcher's, the newsagent's and the grocer's, there is much more discussion of the weather and the cycle race than of the event that has been organised by the municipal council for 13 July.

This has, however, been a long time in the planning. At the end of the winter, the mayor was able to persuade the town council to agree unanimously to honour the memory of those victims of the Nazis who had been living in the commune during the last war and who have been almost entirely forgotten. Their names, only recently emerging from oblivion, would be inscribed on a stone tablet, like those of the soldiers, Resistance fighters and hostages killed between 1940 and 1945. The names would not be included on the war memorial but on a plaque to be attached to the wall of the *mairie*. At the very spot where the group of women and children had gathered after their arrest sixty years before.

The ceremony is not at all like those that are so popular in this part of the country where people happily proclaim their attachment to the past, where they boast of having longer memories than elsewhere, and where, in spite of the television, there is still a flourishing degree of ancestor worship. What is happening this summer is completely unprecedented, the honouring of people who were not only outsiders but who have been forgotten by virtually everyone. In effect, it is a ceremony of exhumation. I suspect that the initiative will leave the sceptics cold and disquiet others for whom it is always undesirable to 'stir up the past'.

And I should admit that, like others, I have also had my doubts about the proposal. What purpose is served by the many plaques and monuments one finds throughout the region commemorating the exploits of the Resistance and, most frequently, the summary executions? What purpose will be served by this one, unveiled the day before the country's national holiday, to mark the sixtieth anniversary of events that the vast majority of the population knows nothing about? For how many years will all these monuments remain legible, comprehensible? One day in the future, bewildered archaeologists will perhaps puzzle over the masses of inscriptions present in our towns and rural areas as over a heap of Greek or Roman obelisks. Couldn't it rather be argued that our age suffers from a surfeit of commemorations and memorials? Do we really need another one?

I may have had doubts but they do not last. How can it be right to accept the eradication of the traces of barbarity, to acquiesce in the forgetfulness demanded by the Nazis and perpetrators of other genocides? Last year, after an exhaustive investigation, a local association, working to preserve the memory of the deportees, also arranged to install a plaque, in this case to be placed on the wall of the station in Meymac, the little town closest to Bugeat. It recalls the fact that on 19 April 1944, shortly after the 'week of bloodshed', dozens of people, most of them Jews, were lined up on the platforms there and loaded onto the train that deported them. The list, still incomplete, contains the names of fifty-nine women, men and children, names now saved from collective oblivion, and curious passers-by frequently linger by the plaque, dumbfounded.

The importance of the event on 13 July 2004 resides less in the unveiling of the plaque than in the presence of members of the families of the victims. The initiative was taken by Lucie Fribourg's grandson, Henry Fribourg, who is older now than his grandmother was at the time of her arrest. Having maintained many links with France, where he was born, he had decided two years previously to find out as much as he could about Bugeat, the town his father had mentioned so rarely but always with such horror.

I spoke on the telephone to Henry Fribourg in Tennessee a few weeks after his first, short visit. Speaking a slightly rusty French with a barely perceptible American accent, he told me about his last meeting with his grandparents, an occasion he remembers with photographic immediacy. It was in Marseille in January 1942, at the Hôtel Splendide (the very place where the US special envoy, Varian Fry, had been based in the spring of 1940 while he worked to arrange the passage out of France of numerous artists and intellectuals escaping from the Nazis). He was twelve years old and was about to leave for North Africa and Cuba with his parents and his brothers and sisters. They were all very sad but not particularly worried. The grandparents they were leaving behind surely had nothing to fear, they were both French citizens and the grandfather had served in the French army as an officer in the reserves. In addition to this, they were materially well off and would be able to withstand the difficult times ahead for their country.

As for the rest, yes, of course he *knew*. His grandmother Lucie had been deported via Drancy, had died in Auschwitz, probably gassed soon after her arrival on 15 May 1944. After that first conversation, we often exchanged messages. I was looking forward to reading his autobiography entitled *I Gave You Life Twice*, just published in the United States and already available on the internet, and always liked finding at the end of his email messages the same warning by Mark Twain: 'Whenever you find you are on the side of the majority, it is time to pause and reflect.'

Honorary professor at the University of Tennessee, a specialist in agriculture and the environment, Henry Fribourg is a vibrantly energetic personality and a radical nonconformist. He needs no urging to launch into the story of his family's epic journey during the war, from Marseille to Oran, to Casablanca, to Havana (where they stayed for three years), and finally to the United States, which the family reached only in the spring of 1945. While his grandparents were being hounded out of the south of France and were seeking refuge on the Plateau de Millevaches, where the worst possible fate befell them, he was an excited child discovering the wonders of the Caribbean. When speaking of his grandfather Albert, who died of pneumonia in April 1943 and was buried in the cemetery at Bugeat before the Germans erupted onto the scene a year later, he reiterates again and again that as a result of his grandfather's service as a lieutenant in the army reserve, his family had rights, including the right to unconditional protection by the French state. As though his words could have some retrospective agency. In a photograph of his grandparents, taken before the war, that the grandson displays with pride, Albert and Lucie are standing side by side, a pleasant, well-to-do upper middle class couple, Albert wearing a starched collar and waistcoat, Lucie with matching necklace, brooch and earrings. One of them is looking directly at the camera, the other into the distance.

As a result of recent contact with the family of the former owners of the house where his grandmother stayed, Henry Fribourg has just retrieved some old documents. Among them is a small sheet of paper covered with tightly spaced, even handwriting. Written by Lucie Fribourg herself, the last thing she ever wrote, after her arrest and a few days before her deportation. A letter addressed to her landlady:

> I am permitted to receive one parcel of clothing containing the following items – this parcel should be sent to the following address: U.G.I.F., 120 Boulevard de Belleville, Paris – to be delivered to Mme Fribourg, Drancy Camp. Thank you. Best wishes.
>
> Blouse, nightdress, knickers, corset, vest, stockings, shoes, slippers, safety pins, suspender belt, umbrella, gloves, a scarf, a mirror, a toothbrush, nail brush, toiletries, sewing kit, handkerchiefs, clothes brush, a skirt and good blouse or a dress for the same purpose, dressing gown, dishcloths.

The care expended on this list of clothes and urgently needed objects reveals that anxiety had not yet extinguished hope. Like the majority of other Jewish people incarcerated in the camp at Drancy, Lucie Fribourg could not have imagined what the next stage was going to be. The precious parcel, sent by her landlady to the UGIF, the Jewish support organisation, would never have reached her. By 26 April, Lucie Fribourg was already on her way to Auschwitz in one of the sealed wagons of convoy 72. By that time she would certainly have realised that her umbrella, gloves and dressing gown would be out of place, decidedly superfluous.

In spite of the competing attraction of the Tour de France, a hundred or so people gather between the church and the *mairie*, late in the afternoon, sixty years later. Henry Fribourg, in the grip of deep emotion, speaks about his grandmother, killed because of her 'race', deported to Auschwitz 'for having committed the unforgivable crime of being a Jew, even though also French and a free woman'. He has researched his family history and found that the family had been settled in Lorraine from 'at least' 1640, and over the centuries several of his forebears had undertaken military service under the French flag. His great grandfather, Lucie's father, Auguste Ach, had himself served in the French army for six years, 'promoted to the rank of grenadier-fusilier on 24 June 1859 in the 26th Infantry Regiment'. Henry Fribourg provides the precise details as though to a committee of enquiry, as though proof of patriotism and good citizenship were still required. He castigates the 'baseness of the Occupiers and their lackeys', the joint responsibility of the Vichy government and the Germans, whom he continues to refer to as 'Boches', a term that we have gradually learned not to use any more. Through his tears, his anger is implacable.

For her part, Francine Uhlmann, the granddaughter of Clara, gives the impression of having come to terms with her anger a long time ago. She is an optimistic, independent and strong-willed woman, discovered by astonishing good luck as a result of a letter sent to the only Uhlmann listed in the telephone directory for Brussels and Liège (where Clara was born). Two days after my letter was sent, she telephoned me, her voice trembling with emotion. She may have come to terms with her anger but not with her grief. She chooses to speak directly to her grandmother, whom she addresses in the old-fashioned way as 'Grandmama': 'I still miss you, Grandmama, and yet I am now a lot older than you were when you were living here.' What is important for her today is precisely this *here*, the fact that the name of her grandmother should be finally inscribed here, in a commune of France whose name goes back many centuries and was shown on maps long before those of Cassini. A *here* where people live who were born here and whose forebears lie in graves in the cemetery. There will be a mark carved in stone, located in a real place that is physically present on this earth, to counter the annihilation, to undo the confusion and dispersal of the ashes from the furnaces of the crematoria, human remains metamorphosed into mineral fertiliser, calcium, ammonia, carbon and sulphur dioxide.

The speeches continue. The team from the regional television station arrive late, and move unobtrusively into the middle of the small crowd: it will be an unusual item for the seven o'clock news the next day, during this holiday period when weary journalists must dash from commune to commune to record gala days and country fairs. The proceedings begin to drag slightly as each speech has to be translated. Chaim Rozent reads aloud a text in English and Henry Fribourg provides a rough translation. Henry's wife, Claude, a professor of French language and culture at an American university, takes over when tears threaten to overwhelm him. In the Israeli family group, they translate softly to each other in English and Hebrew, moving from one language to the other and back again, struggling to find the words. In order to speak about his father, Chaim chooses to recount what has happened in his family since that terrible April day. It's as though he has just come back after a brief absence of sixty years. His two sisters, Shifra and Hanna, who were called Sylvia and Anna at that time, hold each other tightly.

> Our father was murdered because he was a Jew and a member of the Resistance. For all these years, we, his children, have never been told the truth about what happened here. We grew up knowing that we had lost our father but unable to grieve this loss or even to alleviate our mother's suffering.

Before unveiling the plaque, the mayor makes a sombre and dignified speech in which he argues that the time has come 'to reinstate the truth of our history', to 'make good a historic lapse of memory'. Insisting that it is every citizen's duty to be vigilant and to refuse all equivocation, he quotes Bernanos: 'People tell you that freedom cannot die, but this is not so, in the hearts of men freedom can indeed die, and you need to remember this.' The tricolour flag falls from the plaque, made of pink Ambiaud granite, and the names of the victims are read aloud.

Among them is one called André Drouaine. Originally from Metz, he was working for one of the companies constructing the dam on the river Vézère, and he was twenty years old. He was arrested and deported in the middle of winter 1943 because of the links he had with young people of his own age in the maquis or attempting to avoid the STO,[1] and he died two years later, in January 1945, in Koenigstein, a little town near Frankfurt. He was probably not Jewish. But it feels entirely right that his name should be listed here among those who were arrested simply because they were Jews.

The list is not complete: a space has been left after the last name so that others can be added if necessary.

The children and grandchildren of the victims want to make contact with anyone who might still have any memory of their deceased relatives. The smallest anecdote assumes epic proportions. With photographic equipment and video cameras slung over their shoulders, the little group spreads out into the town. What began as a pilgrimage soon resembles an excursion, gives rise to comic encounters and misunderstandings.

Deep emotion soon takes over again. The Rozent children search for any trace of the presence of their father in the former barber's salon where he had worked. But the shop has recently been turned into a dining room and no longer contains any reminders of the barber's salon it once was, with mirrors, swivel chairs, washbasins and display shelves of cosmetics. This is, however, the very same glass panelled door that Jem, never forgetting that his real name was Chaim, pushed open as he raced to save his family on the morning of 6 April. While the barber's widow describes the scene, recalling the repeated warnings given by her husband, Shifra and Hanna look intently at her face, trying to see beneath the wrinkles and white hair some trace of the young woman who helped their mother on more than one occasion during the winter of 1943. They hug and kiss her as though she were a long lost relative.

There is so much to show as the layout of the town is virtually identical to what it was half a century ago. The number of new buildings completed since the war can be counted on the fingers of two hands. This is a euphemism to say that here, on the Plateau, economic development has hardly been rampant. What still remains to be done is to pinpoint precisely the houses where the victims lived. The task is easy for Lucie Fribourg and Clara Uhlmann. The two ladies had found accommodation in the same street, in two newly built houses that broke with the traditional style of rural housing – *villas*, as they were described at the time with a touch of snobbery. The grandchildren, now themselves grown old, are delighted to be photographed in front of the houses, standing at the top of the front steps or under a glass awning.

The last lodging of the Rozent family turns out to be quite difficult to find. A clumsy translation leads the children to think that their parents used to live in the finest house in the town, an eighteenth-century manor house, now owned by the commune, where lunch has been arranged for all the visitors. They rush in, are fulsome in their praise of the monumental fireplace, the huge '*bassière*',* the granite flagged floor, they caress the stones and take dozens of photographs until the misunderstanding becomes apparent and they are disabused. Then the mayor takes them to another house which, it is thought, must be the one where their father, his brother, his wife and their children had lived. More photographs, renewed intensity of looking, renewed emotion. But, deceived by an annoying similarity between the names of two properties, we discover that we have again made a mistake. No, it is not here but a few hundred metres further up the main street. People burst out laughing, the pilgrimage begins to feel more like a party. The children do not take offence. Finally reaching the correct location, we find one of the few new houses built in the town centre. It has been built on the site of the little cottage inhabited by the Rozent family at the beginning of 1944. The cottage was demolished thirty years ago, and nothing is left of it. Alternating between hysterical laughter and stupefaction, the Israeli family hesitates this time before taking any photographs. Shifra, the eldest, with her beautiful passionate face, cannot hide her grief: she was only four years old when she lived in this place but she had hoped it

---

* A local word for the stone sinks used in the kitchens of old houses in the days before running water.

was here that she would find the buried image of a garden that haunts her dreams. I think I know what she is talking about. She and I share, deeply buried in our memories, nebulous images of the same rural world as seen by a child. I tell her that we must have walked past each other as toddlers on these same footpaths or, in the summer, on the banks of the Vézère, perhaps we played and prattled together. She bursts out laughing.

Two places make more of an impression on the children from Israel. Firstly, the station at Pérols situated on the outskirts of the town, just where fields and woodland take over, the station where their parents and other foreign Jews from the south of France arrived one night in January 1943. The modern looking railcars that continue to use the line have not stopped at the station for many years and the station itself has been sold to some Dutch people. Disturbed by our curiosity, their dog barks incessantly.

Then, on the main road to Limoges, at the point where the highway intersects with the asphalted track leading up to the farm called L'Omelette. This is the spot where their father was murdered. Here, on this patch of grass, is where his body lay. The place is no longer in the shade as the old beech trees that lined the highway were recently cut down. But the birdsong and the crystal-clear sound of water lapping in the river still accentuate the silence.

To the children of Chaim, the grandson of Lucie Fribourg, the granddaughter of Clara Uhlmann, who have all travelled from so far away this summer to rediscover the past, how is it possible to explain these events that took place more than half a century ago? Is it sensible even to try to explicate something that was totally insane, to attempt to reconstruct a historical narrative in such meticulous detail? Perhaps it would have been wiser to leave them alone and let them each grieve in their own way. Perhaps the silence should have been enough.

But how could one not respond to their insistent questioning? From their childhood onwards, they have been searching in vain for answers; they no longer wish to be comforted, they wish only to know why and how their family tragedy came about in this place far removed from the turbulence of the world, in the spring of 1944, while the war still raged but when peace was so near. They are in a hurry to discover the truth, as feverish as journalists working on a contemporary investigation. As feverish as journalists but as anxious as lost children.

When they all meet that evening at the hotel, they swap stories like tourists returning from an excursion. The Americans, the Belgian woman, the Israelis do not come from the same background, they have no history in common, but they share this particular event that dates back sixty years. Several hours later, they have worked out a scheme to come back, bringing their own children and grandchildren. They are dreaming of a chain of memory that will continue forever.

The present day comes to the fore again. They talk about France, so close and yet so foreign. The Rozent family is amazed by the kindness and understanding shown them by people they have met over the course of the day, because the Israeli media never miss an opportunity to report that the land of Dreyfus is once again swamped by a wave of virulent anti-Semitism. Claude and Henry Fribourg for their part find in Francine Uhlmann a kindred spirit. As militant activists for human rights, they are delighted to discover in her a comparable determination to fight the neoconservatives who wish to take over the world. The tears shed earlier in the day have dried.

At the end of the evening, Francine Uhlmann takes out of her suitcase with infinite care a little bound volume whose pages are covered with such exquisite calligraphy that one can hardly believe at first that it is a handwritten manuscript. It belonged to her grandmother Clara who had been given it many years ago by a cousin who was deeply in love with her. In order to express his feelings, the boy had written these poems and copied them out himself in beautiful copperplate, and had then created a precious binding for the volume. It is a unique and enchanting object, a poignant reminder of an age long past. The young lover refers to his cousin as 'my dear companion', an enterprising and forward looking girl for the period, and he attempts to dissuade her from going abroad to improve her foreign-language skills. Every page ends with the same verse that is repeated as a kind of refrain:

> Why are you going to Germany,
> Why are you leaving for Germany?
> Don't stay away in Germany,
> Oh! don't go to Germany.

This little volume of innocent, teasing poems addressed to a young girl dreaming of visiting Germany is dated 1892. Clara was sixteen years old and was too eager to see the world to heed the prayers of the boy who loved her. So that was when she made her first visit to Germany, and she came home full of the kind of enthusiasm that only adolescents experience.

Our pasts overlap and interconnect.

The day after the children of the Jewish victims had traced their deceased relatives is another beautiful summer day. The little cosmopolitan group takes great pleasure in filming the ceremony for Bastille Day, the Fourteenth of July, at which flagpoles are set up around the bust of Marianne and police and firemen form the guard of honour, standing rigidly to attention. Later on, at peace now and happy to talk, the group breaks up and they go their separate ways in search of souvenirs to take home to their children and friends. While they are scattered throughout the town, a tall fellow makes a sudden appearance. He is about fifty years old and talks to everyone he meets. He speaks German and very little French. He explains that he lives in Berlin, is originally from Poland, and that he is spending a few days of his summer holiday camping at the local campsite. But if he has come to this exact place, it is for a reason that has little to do with tourism: his father had been forced to join the Wehrmacht and was said to have been killed near here at the end of the war. He turns to me and asks me, '*Kennen Sie zufällig ein deutsches Grab in der Nähe?*' (Would you by any chance know if there is a German grave in the neighbourhood?). The story goes on and begins again, yet another story.

From One Memorial to Another

Paris, Haute-Corrèze, Berlin, Winter 2004–Summer 2007

I STILL HAVE TO VISIT THE 'WALL OF NAMES' THAT has recently been constructed at the Memorial to the Shoah in the Marais district of Paris. I wanted to go soon after its inauguration but was deterred by the enormous crowds overflowing into the Rue Geoffroy-l'Asnier; metal barriers had been installed on the road by the police just like on the days when there is a demo.

There is an icy wind on this morning in early December and the crowds are significantly smaller, but there is nevertheless a group of a hundred or so, lining up opposite the primary school that now, like all other state schools in Paris, displays on its façade a black plaque recalling that Jewish pupils were taken from this school with the 'active collusion' of the Vichy government. A group of tough looking, black-clad security guards, employed by the Memorial, stand outside, stamping their feet to keep warm. They are equipped with earpieces and have miniature microphones tucked into their gloves, and they scrutinise every visitor, ready to intervene forcefully if necessary. The security gate, bristling with electronic devices, lets one visitor through at a time. Contemporary forms of violence proliferate endlessly and haunt these places dedicated to the memory of the victims of past violence.

There is little talking in the queue. People are mostly concerned to protect themselves from the biting wind and the sleet that has begun to fall. I suspect that I am not the only one to think it must have felt a lot colder on the assembly grounds of the camps and on the endless plains traversed during the 'death march' and, in the same moment of thought, to realise that any such comparison is inappropriate.

A few words start a tentative conversation. Next to me, a couple smilingly express approval that there are so many people here. These two have come a long way, from the south of France where they live, and although they are complaining about the bitter cold, they have no intention of giving up. Like many other visitors, myself included, they are keen to check the presence of one or more names among those engraved on the famous wall, covering it from top to bottom, that record the 76,000 Jews who were arrested in France and deported. The name this couple has come to find is that of the father of the very pleasant woman to whom I have been talking and who has already told me:

> My father was arrested in the street during the round-up of the Vel d'Hiv,[1] probably as a result of a tip-off. He was a handsome man, strong and well built. I was always told that he died in Drancy and I believed that for a long time until I found out quite recently that he died in Auschwitz, a few days after his arrival in the camp. He had probably protested because he wasn't the type to submit quietly. But I know so little and I may find out something more here.

And she adds, 'Do you think that inside there are people who will help us search for information?' With her hair cut short and dyed red, she looks a lot younger than her age. During the war, she was living in Paris, in the 18th arrondissement. 'Yes, I did indeed wear the yellow star,' she says as though stating the obvious. She wore it to school. There were about ten other Jewish girls in her class.

> Several of them, the foreigners, were arrested. Not me. Whenever we got word that there was to be a raid, my mother and I used to go upstairs to the very top of our block of flats and we would spend the night huddled together on the top step.

They fall silent suddenly, intent on their quest, and I leave them as they make their way towards not one but several high walls of pale stone. The names are listed in alphabetical order and according to the year of deportation. 'My' people must be among the last, all grouped together in the year 1944. I say 'mine' as though, through long acquaintanceship with their ghosts, I have finally been welcomed into their families.

Even in death there is unequal treatment and chance plays a part: the most favoured victims are those whose names are inscribed at eye level, otherwise one has to step back, crane one's neck, change spectacles, crouch down, even kneel on the ground. When the names are within reach, they can be stroked, touched, caressed; it is a different thing entirely. I have read in the newspapers that the 'Wall of Words' is a 'virtual cemetery'. In fact it is the complete opposite: a cemetery that is hard, smooth and sensitive, responsive to changes in the weather and in the airflow that modifies the temperature of the stone, making it lighter or darker according to the position of the sun and the clouds. It is only the names themselves that remain undisturbed, unchanging.

In spite of the cold that numbs the fingers, I follow what others around me are doing, and tick off on a sheet of paper each time I find one of the names I am seeking. All of 'mine' are indeed here, listed with their surname and given name, followed by their date of birth: Fribourg Lucie, Hoch Karola, Izbicka Anna, Izbicka Jeanne, Kleinberg Maryem, Kleinberg Anna, Kleinberg Rosa, Tencer Brana, Tencer Serge, Uhlmann Clara.

They are all here, all those who were brought together in Bugeat late on the morning of 6 April 1944 and transported to Limoges and then to Drancy before being crammed into the sealed cattle wagons of convoy number 72. Women and children of all sorts and conditions, of various nationalities, all arrested for the sole reason that they were Jews. This wall, which bears the names of all those who were deported in the 'convoys of death' – including the few who managed to survive – is a bulwark against oblivion. The ashes of all the bodies cremated in the ovens were systematically dispersed precisely so that the solution would indeed be 'final', so that it could never be undone, and there would be no coming back, even in words. Yet in spite of the Nazis' obsessive desire to cover up their crimes, and their methodical attempts, right up to the last days of a war they had already lost, to carry the task to fruition, the names flood back, become a physical presence embedded in the real world. Here in Paris, over there in a little town in the Limousin, further afield in Jerusalem, and in many other places.

After sixty years, they have emerged from what was a temporary void. The letters, carved into the thickness of the stone, constitute tangible proof that each of the 76,000 surnames lined up in columns here represents one human being who had been a child before becoming an adult, an individual who had had a father and a mother, a human being who is hereby regaining his or her place in a family tree. Some people may find this small comfort. It is, in fact, nothing short of miraculous, in that it constitutes a victory over a whole programme that aimed at systematic obliteration. The whiteness of the Jerusalem stone with which the walls have been built and the elegant font used for the inscriptions ensure that in any case this is the opposite of a monument dedicated to hatred and bitterness. This is a place at peace with itself. Nearby, some visitors cannot resist taking out their mobile phones, speaking quietly to call a relative or someone close, simply to tell them that they have just found the name of a lost relative. It is as if the call came from beyond the grave. 'Yes, I've checked the date, it is really him, he is right in front of me. I can't get over it. Right in front of me. Can you hear me, do you understand?'

But it is to Serge Klarsfeld that we must return. Through his passion and single-minded determination, he has played a crucial role in identifying and accounting for the multitudes of the unburied dead. His commitment to them became his life's work as it did also for his wife, Beate. At the beginning of the 1970s, when I was working for the newspaper *Combat*, I would often see that energetic young German woman in the shabby offices the paper occupied in the Rue du Croissant. I admired but was somewhat bemused by her daring and intransigence; she had recently slapped the German Chancellor Kiesinger, castigating him as a Nazi (which he had in fact been). She used to write incendiary articles for the paper, denouncing the general amnesia and the impunity enjoyed by so many of the former leaders responsible for the Jewish genocide. The opinion pieces by Beate, often published in the front page 'basement' slot, were intended to cause trouble and to hit hard. Her articles jolted us out of our lethargy; they led me to the realisation that people of my generation, and their parents, had often been far too ready to gloss over the worst of the past, or more precisely, her articles made me realise how much had been done so that we should know nothing. From the time of the Liberation and for a long time afterwards, we had in fact adopted the habit of revering the deportees as long as they had been in the

Resistance, and losing sight of, or completely ignoring, the hosts of others, notably the racial deportees. Our history had been tragic but it was to be admirable and heroic, like a story in a picture book.

The Klarsfelds held us to account. Thanks to Beate, Klaus Barbie and several other Nazi leaders were arrested, prosecuted and found guilty. Thanks to Serge, a memorial on paper was published and republished, constantly revised, that huge grey-covered volume to which I have so frequently turned, whose pages, somewhere between typescript and print, are filled with the interminable lists of the victims. The paper memorial is the forerunner of the one made of stone. Peering through the thick lenses that correct his myopia, Serge Klarsfeld has closely examined many thousands of cases and he recalls the precise details of each as though they were members of his own family. But he insists doggedly that the primary task is to find and include all those who have not so far been listed, that even though the executioners have themselves been dead for many years, it is important that they should not have in their grasp a single unknown victim, that every last one must be reclaimed. I am told that, following advice from the network of associations of former deportees, he has just recorded Chaim Rozent as being one of the fifteen hundred or so Jews shot dead in France during the war.

In Auschwitz, in Jerusalem, in Paris and in Bugeat, it will have taken half a century to build a memorial. In Berlin itself, a memorial has been created — intriguing, monumental, magnificent. It occupies an extensive area surrounded by the splendid new skyscrapers which have been built on the site of the former Potsdamer Platz to enable history to start again from zero. The memorial — that does not speak its name — extends as far as the end of the streets where the buildings once stood that housed the government departments responsible for administering the Third Reich's genocide, and is a few hundred metres from Hitler's bunker. My grandchildren, along with many other little Berliners like them, play hide and seek in the vast labyrinth that constitutes the memorial, they climb onto the great blocks of polished, dark stone, and run between the blocks. Guards circulate, trying to prevent this enigmatic place of contemplation being turned into a playground and picnic site. For the moment it seems that their efforts are exhausting rather than effective.

Even more than this impressive memorial located in the heart of a city that was destroyed and is being reborn, even more than the Jewish Museum where, through countless subtle techniques, an attempt is made to make palpable the unsayable of the Shoah, what most moves me in Berlin are the brass medallions attached to the granite flagstones of the pavements in the old town. They are to be found all over the place in certain districts, in front of apartment blocks that escaped the Allied bombing raids, but also in front of new blocks built on the ruins. Each time, the name of the person who lived there before the implementation of the 'final solution', for instance the name of a young girl, her date of birth, date of deportation, date of death or, where this is not known, three question marks. Chosen at random in a street that I came to know well:

Georg Gerson, j.g. 1882, deportiert 1943, ermordert Auschwitz; Hannelore Leske, j.g. 1932, deportiert 1942, Theresienstadt, ???; Marie Scheibe, geb. David, j.g. 1868, deportiert 1942, Theresienstadt, ???

[Georg Gerson, born 1882, deported 1943, murdered Auschwitz; Hannelore Leske, born 1932, deported 1942, Theresienstadt, ???; Marie Scheibe née David, born 1868, deported 1942, Theresienstadt, ???]

At the beginning of 2005, in order to mark the anniversary of the liberation of the camp at Auschwitz on 27 January 1945, the newspapers refrain from using the familiar 'Never Again' headlines. In France and abroad, many papers choose the same headline: 'Auschwitz, 60 years on: the world refuses to forget'. This is not a perfunctory gesture. The last survivors among the deportees, those who had been in their twenties and who know that this anniversary of the liberation of the camp might be their last, are finally breaking their silence. A number have agreed to go back to Auschwitz for the first and the last time. One of them, Sam Braun, admits: 'I never spoke about it to my children because I thought, foolishly, that they should not be enmeshed in my fate.' What he says next is even more significant: 'We all have in us the potential to become an SS if we give in to it, and it's a bold man who says "I would never".' After the trip through the grimy snow of Auschwitz, he is not the only one to come back with similar thoughts.

Simone Veil, the former president of the European Parliament, is one who agreed to go back, accompanied by her children. Speaking to all the heads of state assembled there to commemorate the liberation of the camp, she said what had to be said. She was sixteen years old in the spring of 1944, the same age as Jeanne Izbicka, the niece of Marie Kleinberg, who was arrested in Bugeat on 6 April. Simone Veil left Drancy on convoy 71, Jeanne Izbicka on convoy 72, arriving only a few days later. I know virtually nothing about Jeanne, whose name and existence I discovered from a list held by the Vichy police. I do know, however, that having reached the infamous selection ramp at Auschwitz, because they were no longer children, neither would have been directed to the gas chambers, about which they were totally ignorant. A man signalled with his thumb that they were to turn left, to line up on the good side.

Following a recent request for information addressed to the *mairie* in Metz, I discover that Jeanne was not killed in Auschwitz, that she was among the very few survivors of convoy 72; the local register of births, deaths and marriages confirms that she died in Lorraine in 1970, so she survived for a considerable time, with her deportee number tattooed on her arm. There is something miraculous about her story: close examination of the papers about her I have collected indicate that her date of birth varies from one document to another. According to some, she was born in April 1928, but others give August. In other words, at the time she arrived in Auschwitz she had either just turned sixteen, or she was only fifteen and nine months. The difference is far from negligible. Selection at the entrance to the camp was in the first instance on the basis of age: those over sixteen or eighteen (it varied) could be directed to the work camp rather than the gas chambers, and thus avoid the immediate death to which children and the oldest adults were condemned. Because she was around sixteen years old, because she managed (how?) to make it known that she was over sixteen, because she was fit and healthy, Jeanne was instructed to take the path that led to survival.

The Jewish family from Lorraine to which Jeanne belonged arrived in Bugeat at the beginning of the war, part of the mass exodus. Obeying the edicts issued by the Vichy administration, she was registered as a Jew in 1941. Their residence of nearly four years leaves more traces in people's memories than many others. Several inhabitants of the town point without hesitation to the house on the Rue Nationale where the Kleinberg family lived. They tell me that the father of the family, Joseph, worked on the dam. This was undoubtedly what saved his life because he was working on the construction site at Virolle at the time of the arrests, on the morning of 6 April. A few days after the tragedy, Joseph came back to fetch what was left in the empty house, and he collected together all the children's clothes, the pretty dresses belonging to his two daughters, those belonging to his two nieces, taking care not to leave a single one behind, then he folded them all neatly before packing them with the utmost care into a large suitcase and carrying it away without speaking a word to anyone. Sixty years later, the children who lived in the nearest house have not forgotten the smallest detail of the scene.

But among the fragments of the past that emerge as former neighbours search their memories, one final piece of information bursts like a bombshell: 'Did you know that little Jeanne Izbicka was born profoundly deaf?' Deaf and unable to speak in Auschwitz! A survivor of the camps to whom I put the question is, however, not surprised: during the period of his own deportation, he had himself met a deaf mute. 'People like that could survive provided other people looked after them all the time.' He adds, 'In the camps, all sorts of things were possible.' Marie, now known once again as Maryem, Jeanne's aunt, was in her forties and had probably not been sent to the gas chamber immediately on arrival at Auschwitz. After having lost her own two daughters and having been separated from her youngest niece – all three too young to have avoided being condemned to die from the outset – she was perhaps able to take care of Jeanne, who was so vulnerable, until the very end, until her own death.

Out of the 602 women who left Drancy in convoy 72 and were deported to Upper Silesia, there were only 25 survivors. Jeanne Izbicka was one of them. But about the hell she had endured she was never able to say a word. It could, however, be seen in her eyes.

Fifty Years Later

7 APRIL 1994. ON THAT DAY, THE LAST GENOCIDE OF the twentieth century began. In the heart of Africa, in Rwanda, over a period of three months, it accounted for approximately 800,000 victims, mostly Tutsis, who were slaughtered with machetes and cudgels. A genocide that had been a long time coming and that employed frighteningly basic methods.

6 April 1944, 7 April 1994.

Fifty years, give or take a few hours, separate these two events, which are connected perhaps only in my own mind.

6 April 1944, the Thursday before Easter, in a little town in the Massif Central, a day like any other in the course of the Jewish genocide unleashed by the Nazis. 7 April 1994, a week after Easter, a bloodbath like any other in the streets of the capital of Rwanda: the opening episode of the whirlwind genocide that would engulf the Tutsis.

A vast memorial made of eight massive dark slabs, surrounded by meticulously pruned climbing vines, has just been built on the side of a hill in Kigali.

Jerusalem, Washington, Oradour-sur-Glane, Warsaw, Paris,

Berlin, Srebrenica, Kigali, the Camp des Milles, Pithiviers, Beaune-la-Rolande, Bugeat… There are a great many memorials in the world, some monumental, some modest, all of them designed to make a stand against forgetfulness and indifference, so that the evil should not be repeated.

Postscript to the English Edition

I SPENT SEVERAL YEARS WORKING INTERMITTENTLY ON this investigation focusing on a tiny region, located on the borders of three departments, Corrèze, Creuse and Haute-Vienne, deep in the heart of France. This is the country of my birth. So small a matter, it might be said, and so marginal in relation to the great battles of a world war. Indeed, on more than one occasion I found myself questioning the significance of my one-man investigation into so strictly limited a time and place.

If I never abandoned my research, it was because I very quickly discovered that important elements of local history had been glossed over and buried beneath that other history, the authorised version of the nation's story. Bringing back those who had been buried became for me an urgent task, all the more compelling in that it involved a challenge to prevailing currents of thought.

The well-known Italian author Andrea Camilleri is, like me, fascinated by the coexistence of remembering and forgetting, and he has written a little book about an event that took place over a century and a half ago in his native Sicily, at Porto Empedocle to be precise, which is where he was born. Entitled *La strage dimenticata*

(Palermo: Sellerio Editore, 1984), translated into French as *Un massacre oublié* [A forgotten massacre] (Paris: Le Promeneur, 2002),[1] the book recounts what happened at Porto Empedocle during the winter months of 1847, namely the mass killing of 114 Sicilian convicts at a time when the whole country was in a ferment due to the movement for national liberation. Each of the victims had a surname, a given name and had been baptised. This did not, however, prevent every one of them from disappearing without material trace, unmentioned in any scholarly historical study or even in the family stories handed down from parent to child. That is, until Andrea Camilleri caught hold of them in the nick of time and gave them a second chance at life. Camilleri writes that he is a theatre director, a journalist, an observer of everyday life (is this really a profession?), and most definitely a writer, but he is at pains to explain that he is absolutely not a historian. In his words, 'I do not have the mind of a historian.' His role, as mine, was to reveal that which had been hidden or swallowed up by the onward march of history as it was recounted and transmitted from generation to generation. 'My particular concern is that the second massacre, the one brought about through failure of memory, should be in some way atoned for.'

Camilleri's book ends with the impressive list of all 114 victims, their surnames, given names, age and date of birth 'faithfully' transcribed. To name someone does not bring them back to life, enable them to cheat death. But it does provide evidence of a life, it brings with it proof of that person's existence on earth. And as I pursued my own enquiries I, too, experienced a kind of exultation each time I discovered a list of names. It did not matter whether these lists had been compiled by the gendarmerie, by one or other police force, by a municipal authority, the Vichy government or even the creators of the Memorial of the Shoah. Without these lists, the dead would have no existence, nor would the crimes that were committed. I have come to understand that it is the lists of names that constitute one of the few truly effective methods of countering the Holocaust deniers. Denying that there was a crime is the ultimate realisation of that crime.

I am proud that I have been able to restore to a small number of descendants of victims of the Shoah an individual and family memory of which they were unaware or thought had disappeared forever. Several of these descendants have undertaken a long journey to visit a country whose name they hardly knew, to find the traces that still exist and can be seen and read, to find local inhabitants in whom long-forgotten memories have suddenly been stirred, and more wonderful still, to discover the existence of other members of their own widely scattered families. Among these travellers journeying back in time there is one in particular: Chaim Rozent , son of Jem/Chaim. He is like the hero of a novel, leading this pilgrimage of commemoration, and he has become a dear friend. He is the living personification of the victims' ultimate triumph.

In September 2015, he brought his children and their partners who live close to him in Israel and led them to the grave in the depths of the Limousin countryside where his father was buried after being murdered by the Nazis. Later that day they joined the crowd packed into the church in Bugeat to listen to the most extraordinary concert. For it was on the old violin that had been brought back to France from Israel for the first time in seventy years, the violin that had been handed down in the Rozent family from father to son in Poland, brought to Antwerp and kept safe throughout each stage of the family's flight through France and finally to Israel – it was on this violin that Elina Kuperman played the Mourner's Kaddish and the supplication for peace.

In the wake of the book, they came from far away to be present at this memorial concert and to participate in the conference organised to coincide with it. Entitled 'Jewish Memories in the Limousin', the conference took place in a village at the very centre of the Plateau de Millevaches. The direct descendants of the Jewish victims of 6 April 1944 who were able to be present – members of the Rozent family and of Carola Hoch's family – were accorded honorary citizenship of the commune of Bugeat and the surrounding region. The thing I shall remember above all else about the event is the intense expression in the eyes of Jem/Chaim's grandchildren as they watched. Their names are Gal, Inbal, Raanan, Nitzan, Ofer. They live with their families in Israel, several have already reached the age of their grandfather at the time of his murder, and at the discovery of a past that was until now little more than an abstraction, they do not look away.

It must be said that, since this book was published as *Jeudi Saint* in France, there have been many moments of high emotion. As the book reached increasing numbers of readers, so I began to receive more and more corroborative evidence in the form of letters and emails, and sometimes simply in the course of conversations with people I met casually in the street. In French there is a phrase: tongues are loosened. And that is precisely what happened. Dozens of people who had been direct or indirect witnesses began to recount their own personal experiences of the general amnesia that followed the events of 1944. And suddenly, due to the impact of this book, I think it can be said that they have recovered their own memory.

The thing I found out that I certainly was not expecting was the extent of the influx of Jewish people who, from the very beginning of World War II right up until the end, sought refuge in the depths of rural France, in the Massif Central and more particularly in the mountainous country of the Limousin. Even scholars specialising in the study of the region have been unaware of the magnitude of the numbers involved. For a long time it was thought that the persecution of the Jews and the implementation of the policy of extermination of European Jewry was felt far more acutely in urban areas than in the countryside. The reality is quite different.

In nearly every village on the Plateau de Millevaches, there were Jewish families who had sought refuge and who were being spontaneously shielded by the locals in part in response to the region's ancient traditions of hospitality but also, it seems to me, as a result of the values inculcated in the schools of the Third Republic.

While the majority of these Jewish refugees were saved, there were also a great many victims. In addition to those taken on 6 April 1944, who have been brought back symbolically in my home village, I am thinking of all those who were arrested in the immediate vicinity during the last two years of the war. They were either murdered on the spot or deported to suffer the most atrocious deferred death simply because they were Jews. I am thinking of the peat cutters taken from Barsanges, of the groups arrested in Lonzac, in Treignac, in Toy-Viam, in Tarnac, in Lacelle, in Eymoutiers, and in other places. Not to mention the large number taken in Meymac whose terrible story has hardly been touched on in this book and who really deserve their own detailed study. If I cite these hamlets and villages whose names have not gained wide currency, it is as a reminder that history can never be detached from geography.

My cautious estimate is that within a radius of twenty kilometres from Bugeat there were approximately 200 Jewish victims – men, women, children and old people – for whom the Limousin protective shield failed. This is probably greater than the number of resisters who were killed fighting in the region. In relation to the low density of the rural population living at that elevation in the mountains, it represents a very significant loss. It may perhaps be calculated one day that the number of victims of the Shoah taken from the sparsely populated rural areas of France was proportionately higher than in the urban region of Paris.

When a national tragedy of this sort comes to an end, the transition from one political order to the next does not occur without some

final acts of violence. In the immediate aftermath, summary jus-
tice prevailed. A number of suspects were arrested, some women
had their heads shaved, and rumour and suspicion abounded. In
the weeks immediately following the Liberation, some known
collaborators were covertly executed. They remain nameless.
Notwithstanding the fact that the civil authorities carried out their
allotted roles at the time, this is a topic about which, seventy years
later, it is still virtually impossible to speak.

In writing this book, I made a conscious decision to avoid
tackling the double issue of denunciations and of the purge which
began shortly after the events of 6 April 1944. While my inquiry
had led me to search the archives for lists of names of people who
had been taken in the various 'round-ups' and 'sweeps', I never
looked in the same way for a list of those who were 'purged'. If
such a list exists, I believe it would be a short one and that the victims of the purge that occurred in the spring, summer and autumn
of 1944 (I am speaking of those who lost their lives) can probably
be counted on the fingers of two hands. No more than that. I
heard certain names mentioned, and was given rough indications
of place. I do not quote any of these. Firstly, this is because I am
reluctant to establish any kind of parallel between the murder-
ous insanity of the Nazis and a few acts of retaliation by angry
Resistance fighters. But also because these victims have certainly
left descendants, people who are probably the same age as me,
whom I pass in the street. More than one of them, so I am told, has
lived in the belief that his forebear died fighting with the Resistance
and not with the bullet in the head meted out to contemptible traitors. I do not have the legal authority, nor am I sufficiently callous
to demand the exhumation of bodies and forensic examination necessary to establish the ultimate guilt of a few impulsive murderers,
most of them late recruits to the ranks of the Resistance.

This is not, however, the last word on the dead and the disappeared. Buried beneath the ground in this country covered

with meadows and woods and vast stretches of moorland carpeted with gorse and heather, there are still other bodies lying in unmarked graves. I was made aware of the existence of this fact the day after the memorial plaque to the victims of Nazism was unveiled in Bugeat. The first clue was provided by the arrival of the ebullient stranger who turned up unannounced in the middle of the celebrations for 14 July 2004, at the very moment when the national flag was being lowered for the minute's silence. He had come from the east, from the further reaches of Europe, and he confided in an undertone that he was staying at the camping ground, that he knew only a few words of French but that he spoke German, that he suffered from allergies and breathing difficulties, and that he intended to come back on another occasion in order to interview some of the local inhabitants. He was able in effect to convey to the people to whom he spoke so briefly that he, too, was carrying out an inquiry and that he, too, was looking for the grave of his father.

The appearance of this son seeking the grave of his soldier-father is all the more troubling because the stranger has to this day never returned. It is as though he realised his quest to be futile and so put it out of his mind after a good night's sleep. But I have never forgotten the fleeting apparition occurring at the very moment we were gathered together to mourn the Jewish victims who had forever been deprived of a grave. In lieu of a tombstone, our ceremony restored the names and given names that had been theirs before the gas chambers. The incident suggested a grotesque parallel between the victims and their persecutors, doomed to disappear without trace or memorial.

On a number of occasions since the publication of *Jeudi Saint*, I have come close to the hint of an admission and have attempted to take it further in conversation with former Resistance fighters – those who are among the last who are still living and who are sufficiently closely related to my family to permit the subject to be raised at all. Each time I have been met with a wall of silence. Not a denial, just silence. The most explicit response I have received has been a weary, evasive look and a vague gesture towards the thick woods and heathland that cover the Plateau, indicating a remote and unmarked spot where proof of such deeds may possibly have been hidden. Perhaps forever (or perhaps not).

The modest scope of my investigation has left a number of leads still to be followed, a number of unanswered questions. I do not believe that this is due to undue caution on my part or laziness. It is rather because there are certain chapters in the local history that have not yet come to fruition, because the story is still unfolding, will never be finished. And it is also an invitation to others, here and elsewhere, to continue the work of remembering, to dig deeper in the areas that they feel deserve it and attempt to bring answers to questions that shift and change as they are transmitted from one generation to the next. Seventy years after these events, young people want to know what happened. Foreigners who have come to live in the region are also curious. Foremost among these are the British citizens who have moved to the area in such numbers, buying up disused farmhouses in which they set up small businesses, or opening delightful bed and breakfast guest houses.

The response received by this book in France has confirmed, if confirmation were needed, that there are many different ways to write history and a number of different sorts of history. Alongside the textbook history taught in schools and promoted by those in power, are the marginal, the local, the dissident, the partisan. These are histories that are in some sense cobbled together from pirated fragments. In so far as they reject the dominant *story telling*,* these other histories continue to open up new fields of

---

* In English in the original. [Note from the translator]

enquiry, reveal unsuspected leads, and amplify our present knowledge with facts that have hitherto been suppressed, rejected or simply forgotten. They aspire neither to establish nor to convey the whole story. More than anything, they resemble the work of those old women in the country who, in days gone by, used to spend their time endlessly patching and repatching the sheets that had formed part of their dowry, keeping them neatly piled in big linen presses in their bedrooms. Amateur and local histories are a mixture of emotion and reason. They add depth and complexity to our understanding of the past. It is naturally among histories of this sort that the investigation recounted in *Jeudi Saint* finds its place.

As I write the last lines of this final chapter destined for English-speaking readers, how could I not express my profound gratitude to Gay McAuley for the enthusiasm which which she undertook the translation of *Jeudi Saint* (now *One Day in France*), and for the part she has played in the life of this book? The historical investigation in which I have been involved for the last ten years has indeed become a little bit her own. To the extent that I find myself thinking that this book is the work of two hands…

JEAN-MARIE BORZEIX
PARIS, JANUARY 2016

Final Note from the Translator

THE RELATIONSHIP BETWEEN TRANSLATOR AND author is very special, at least as far as the translator is concerned, for no other reader or critic spends as long pondering every detail of a text or feels they have acquired such privileged access to the mind of the author. The experience of Alice B. Toklas, as reported by Gertrude Stein, is pertinent here:

> I always say that you cannot tell what a picture really is or what an object really is until you dust it every day and you cannot tell what a book is until you type it or proof-read it. It then does something to you that only reading can never do.[1]

I think that this apparently whimsical remark contains a profound wisdom that applies also to the translator's craft, for translators are necessarily obsessed with the material substance of the text and with the weight of each word and punctuation mark and quirk of syntax. The deeper understanding of the work that they reach comes from this obsessive lingering with the surface features of the writing, like Alice with her duster. They have to follow step by step the author's own writerly trajectory and it is not surprising that they may come to feel a complex sense of shared parenthood in relation to the resulting text.

This has certainly been my experience in translating *Jeudi Saint*, an experience that has been greatly enriched by the generosity of Jean-Marie Borzeix, who has always recognised and encouraged my emotional and intellectual involvement in the story he is telling in this book. Indeed, I am writing this note at his request because he wanted there to be some record of the way the translation came about, of the reason why a retired academic from Australia felt so strongly that the book should be made accessible to English-speaking readers, and of the road we have travelled since 2008 as the story he told has continued to expand. His book is less an account of something that happened seventy years ago and more like a stone thrown into a pond, stirring the mud at the bottom and causing ripples of effect on the surface. I think that, for Jean-Marie, the fact that I took the initiative in seeking permission to translate the book into English is yet another ripple, part of the story of the book's effect.

He told me that he began writing what would become *Jeudi Saint* when the editors of a proposed volume of local history invited him to contribute a chapter recounting the well-known story of the four men from L'Echameil who were shot by the Nazis on Holy Thursday 1944.[2] It was when he was researching this chapter that he first heard about the mysterious fifth man shot that day, a man whose death was not commemorated in the annual ceremony honouring the four local heroes, and whose grave he eventually found in the cemetery of a neighbouring commune. Then, almost by accident, he discovered that ten more people were taken from the village on the same day, women and children, the youngest only three years old, refugees who had been evacuated to the village and had been living there for months. But these people were deported and murdered in Auschwitz, they have no grave, and they had no memorial or place in the collective memory of the village until Jean-Marie started to ask questions. His book is, in effect, a memorial for them.

When I first read *Jeudi Saint* in the summer of 2008, I was moved as much by the story of Jem/Chaim and the other victims as by the way the commune of Bugeat was responding in the present to these revelations about the past. The principal reason I wanted to ensure it was made accessible to English-speaking readers was that it seemed to me such an exemplary instance of the major cultural shift that has been occurring in France over the last twenty to thirty years. The traumatic experiences of World War II were followed in France by a long period during which the pressing need to heal the wounds caused by the realities of defeat, occupation, collaboration and betrayal led to the reality being displaced by a new narrative of heroic resistance and endurance. More perplexing is the fact that the new narrative contained virtually no mention of the internment and deportation of Jews, the vast majority of whom were killed in the Nazi death camps.[3] Political prisoners, forced labourers and prisoners of war returning from the German camps found that no one really wanted to hear about their experiences either. Hélène Bolleau, who had smuggled weapons and undertaken dangerous liaison activities for the Resistance when still a schoolgirl and who survived the hell of Auschwitz for more than two years, was invited after her return home to talk about the camps at a village gathering. She was interrupted by a man who said that if things had been as bad as she claimed, she would not have survived. As Caroline Moorehead recounts this heartbreaking story, Hélène Bolleau went home and 'cried for three days; then she stopped talking'.[4]

Some people were silenced, others chose silence because they could not find the words to express the enormity of what had been done to them or because they wanted to protect their families from such unbearable knowledge. And of course there were others who kept quiet because they were ashamed of what they had done, or failed to do, or because they feared retribution. The inability or refusal to speak on the part of concentration camp survivors finds an echo in the experience of survivors of some of the other terrible wars and mass killings of the twentieth century. Soldiers returning from the trenches of World War I, for example, or even survivors of the bombing of Hiroshima and Nagasaki were frequently unwilling to speak about their experience afterwards even to their families, sometimes only breaking their silence at the end of their lives, often telling a grandchild what they could never bring themselves to tell a son or daughter or spouse.

These kinds of silence do not explain what Jean-Marie here calls the 'general amnesia' that seems to have affected the whole country in relation to what happened to the Jews during the war in France but they clearly feed into and facilitate that amnesia. Anthropologist W. E. H. Stanner, speaking in another context, identified what he called 'a cult of forgetfulness practised on a national scale',[5] and his insight can also be applied to what happened in France in the decades following the war, where the political, intellectual and cultural authorities seem in retrospect to have colluded in ignoring what had happened to the Jews and the French government's own complicity in this. It is no accident that I am citing an anthropologist here as anthropology is perhaps the only discipline that can elucidate the complex mechanisms at work in a society in the grip of such generalised forgetting. A personal anecdote might help to illustrate the intangible way it permeated people's lives. In the 1960s I was a student, living at different times in Strasbourg and Paris, and I knew that one of my friends had been hidden in the country as a child during the war, that her grandparents had been deported, and that the family of another friend had been destroyed and she had been brought up in an orphanage. My friends did not exactly make a secret of these things and yet I seem to have expressed no curiosity to know more. However extraordinary it seems to me now, the terrible events of the recent past were things that were known but somehow not known by their friends, known about but relegated to the background, hidden in plain sight.

As Stanner's work shows, however, such national forgetfulness does eventually get challenged even though this may take a considerable time. In the case of France, it was more than twenty-five years before the amnesia began to be challenged when people born during and after the war started asking questions, breaking the silences, and attempting to bring to the surface what lay beneath the myth-making that had served the national interest for so long. *Jeudi Saint* is part of this profound shift in collective awareness that has been occurring in France as memoirs published in the immediate aftermath of the war and then 'forgotten' are reissued, dedicated volunteers comb the archives and run websites designed to assist people to trace what happened to their relatives, and a host of other works, fictional and documentary, scholarly and journalistic, have helped create a new understanding of what really happened during the so-called 'dark years' of the Occupation.

The response that *Jeudi Saint* received, hinted at by Jean-Marie in the postscript he has written for this English translation, is an indication of the part the book is playing in this complex and painful process. Many people have written to him to add a detail, corroborate a fact, or express their amazement that their country's part in the attempted extermination of European Jewry should have been swept under the carpet for so long. Descendants of the victims, who have spent their whole lives not knowing and not daring to ask, have spoken of their profound emotion at discovering some part of the truth. I have myself experienced the thrill that is felt when a photograph of one of the victims is discovered in an old box of papers or another fact comes to light, for every detail is a triumphant assertion of their life in the face of the Nazis' attempt to obliterate them utterly. Before the publication of the book in 2008, the annual ceremony of remembrance, held in the village on 6 April, referred only to the heroes and martyrs of the Resistance and made no mention of the Jews arrested and deported that day. Things are very different now and not only are the Jewish victims acknowledged by the *maire* in his speech every year on 6 April, but on the last Sunday of that month, France's national day of remembrance for the victims of deportation, the people of Bugeat gather in a special ceremony to honour the eleven deportees whose names, together with that of Chaim Rozent, are engraved on the stone plaque, now prominently displayed on the wall of the *mairie*.

What I did not realise when I sought permission from Jean-Marie Borzeix in 2008 to translate his book into English was that this would be just the beginning of a long and emotionally compelling journey, that I would come to care so deeply about each of the victims, or that I would meet some of their descendants and be made aware of how the terrible violence of that day is still resonating in people's lives. On a recent visit to Bugeat, as I walked around the old school playground where the German soldiers tethered the stolen cow, past the house where the barber shop used to be, and along the '*turgotière*' where Jem hoped to avoid arrest, it seemed to me that the streets and squares of this very ordinary village were still alive with the presence of the people and events described in *Jeudi Saint*. While this is in part due to Jean-Marie's skill as a story teller, it is also evidence of the way places function to hold memory. The book is a necessary trigger but the place itself then becomes a powerful part of a collective memory system. The English translation makes it possible for this memory process to spread even further afield, hopefully throughout the English-speaking world, but it will always be centred on Bugeat.

*

Many people must be thanked for their contributions to the publication of this book, first and foremost the publisher I.B.Tauris and, specifically, Senior Editor Joanna Godfrey, whose enthusiasm and commitment from the outset have been heartwarming. I am also grateful to her team of highly professional collaborators, in particular Sophie Campbell, David Inglesfield and Alex Billington, who have presided over the book's production with exemplary skill, and to David Cox, who made the excellent maps. It has been a pleasure to work with them all. Thank you also to Caroline Moorehead, who has drawn on her own extensive research into the history of the Resistance in France in order to provide an introduction that English-speaking readers will find extremely useful.

David Cesarani is, sadly, no longer with us so cannot be thanked in person for his suggestions about publishers but I would like to place on record nevertheless my appreciation of the help he so unstintingly gave to scholars who approached him. Much support and encouragement also came from former colleagues in Australia, in particular from distinguished translators Julie Rose and Mabel Lee in Sydney and Brian Nelson in Melbourne as well as from Esther Allen in New York and Judith Landry in London. Ivor Indyk, also in Sydney, read sample chapters and gave encouragement at a crucial time, and all of them made me aware how much help translators give each other. Finally, to Barry Thomas who introduced me both to *Jeudi Saint* and its author, a special thank you.

This translation is dedicated to Cécile Gros, deported in convoy 48, February 1943, and to Suzanne Zadoc-Kahn, deported in convoy 62, November 1943, grandmothers to two of my dearest friends who are now grandmothers themselves.

GAY MCAULEY
LONDON, JANUARY 2016

Notes

Preface

1   The canton is a unit of administration in the French system of local government and it consists of a number of communes, each with its elected mayor. Cantons are grouped into departments, each one headed by a prefect appointed by the central government. The names of these administrative units have been retained, albeit in slightly anglicised form, because there are no direct equivalents in regional administration in English-speaking countries. The *mairie* is the administrative centre of the commune and here, too, the French term has been retained. [Note from the translator]

L'Echameil

1   Service du Travail Obligatoire [forced labour in Germany]. Under the Vichy government, young men who refused to go to Germany and undertake this forced labour were designated '*réfractaires*' [recalcitrants].

2   Each unit of the Brehmer Division was made up of forty or so soldiers from the Wehrmacht (German army) together with a dozen Waffen SS who undertook the 'dirty work'. The latter were particularly responsible for the deportation of Jews and for guard duties in concentration camps. They wore the skull and crossbones insignia on the sleeve of their uniform.

Living Testimony

1   Charles Maurras (1868–1952), author and political activist, founder of the anti-Semitic and extreme right-wing movement Action Française, and a prominent supporter of the Vichy government. [Note from the translator]

Jem

1   All the foreign refugees who had been forcibly relocated from the south of France when the Allies landed in North Africa in November 1942 were obliged to register with the police, their identity papers (essential for getting ration cards) were marked with a 'J' if they were Jewish, and they were not permitted to move house without notifying the police. [Note from the translator]

The Future of the Past

1   There is considerable variation in spelling and transliteration of names in the records but Abraham Halgzjait/Halgzait are presumably the same person.
2   See Appendix pp. 157–61.
3   See Appendix pp. 162–5.
4   Among the many letters I received when this book was published in France was one from M. Georges Panker (a retiree living in Paris) who informed me that he, too, had been hidden in the Corrèze as a child and he provided the following information about other members of his family: Brana Tencer was his mother's older sister. Her son, Serge, born in 1940 in Brive, was thus his first cousin. Mother and child arrived in Drancy on 13 April 1944 and were deported in convoy 72 at the end of that month. They never returned.

A Beautiful Summer

1   Service du Travail Obligatoire [forced labour in Germany]. It is thought that some 650,000 French citizens were conscripted and sent to labour camps in Germany between 1942 and 1944. Malnutrition and harsh working conditions led to a high death toll among these workers, perhaps as high as 35,000. [Note from the translator]

From One Memorial to Another

1   A mass arrest of Jewish people in Paris carried out by French police on 16 and 17 July 1942, named for the indoor cycle track (Vélodrome d'Hiver) to which victims were taken before being deported to Auschwitz. [Note from the translator]

Postscript to the English Edition

1 Notwithstanding Camilleri's fame as the author of the Inspector Montalbano mysteries, this book does not seem to have been translated into English. [Note from the translator]

Final Note from the Translator

1 Gertrude Stein, *The Autobiography of Alice B. Toklas* (Harmondsworth: Penguin Books, 1966), p. 124.

2 The closest English translation of Jeudi Saint is Holy Thursday. Through his choice of title, Jean-Marie draws attention to his perception that the horror of the atrocity was compounded for the devout villagers by the fact that it was perpetrated on the day before Good Friday, the most solemn and holy in the Christian calendar. The English title, chosen by the publishers, elides the religious significance but has other strengths.

3 Of the 76,000 Jewish people authoritatively estimated to have been deported from France by the Nazis, only 2,500 returned. See also Jacques Semelin's analysis, in *Persécutions et Entraides dans la France Occupée* (Paris: Les Arènes-Seuil, 2013), of what he calls 'the French enigma', namely the fact that, despite the persecution, three quarters of the pre-war Jewish population of France managed to survive.

4 Caroline Moorehead, *A Train in Winter* (London: Vintage Books, 2012), p. 308.

5 Stanner's work concerned the way white Australia had erased Aboriginal people from its consciousness in the years following independence in 1901, an erasure that was still going on when he wrote these influential lectures in 1968. See W.E.H. Stanner, *After the Dreaming* (Sydney: Australian Broadcasting Commission, 1969).

Appendix

This appendix reproduces two important documents found in the archives of the department of Corrèze:

1. A list of all foreigners living within the boundary of the administrative division (Departmental Archives, Corrèze, Call number: 529W51), taken from a census conducted by the Bugeat brigade of the National Gendarmerie in August 1943.

2. A report dated 18 April 1944 from the Prefect of Corrèze to the Head of Government, Vichy, concerning 'arrests carried out by the German authorities'. An English translation of the document is presented on the facing pages.

12ᵉ Légion de Gendarmerie.

Compagnie de la Corrèze.

Section d'Ussel.

Brigade de Bugeat?
-:-:-:-:-:-:-:-:-:-

LISTE de tous les étrangers en résidence sur le territoire de la circonscripti

Nom et prénoms	Date et lieu de naissance	Nationa-lité.	Commune de résidence.	Observa-tions.
ASSI(Pietro)	19/2/1904 à Lazize(Italie)	Italienne	Bugeat.	
RASSI(née Pupays(Lina)	18/8/1924 à Chiasseklis (Italie)	-do-	-do-	
BERROGAIN(Laita José)	2/4/1916 à Biota(Espagne)	Espagnole	-do-	
JERBOS(François)	4/5/1900 à Abellia(-do-)	-do-	-do-	
CIVICO(Juan)	11/11/1906 à La Carolina (Espagne)	-do-	-do-	
FRANCO(José)	12/4/1901 à Benabarry(Es-pagne)	-do-	-do-	
GODINO,née Morizzio Thérèse)	23/11/1873 à Canavès(Ita-lie)	Italienne	-do-	
GOMEZ,née Del Pozo (Maria)	14/10/1912 à Madrid(Espa-gne)	Espagnole	-do-	
RATTI(Eugène)	27/10/1889 à Cairo-Montério(to)Italie)	Italienne	-do-	
JIMENEZ(José)	9/1/1915 à Véles Blanca (Espagne)	Espagnole	-do-	
KLOCEK(Ignace)	14/11/1907 à Wyzsa(Pologne)	Polonaise	-do-	
KAPLAN,néSamson(Sarza (J.)	15/10/1906 à Warta(Pologne)	-do-	-do-	
LORENZO(Secundo)	23/5/1917 à Penaroga(Es-pagne)	Espagnole	-do-	
MARCINKOWSKI(Joseph)	21/2/1918 à Sterkrade(Alle-magne)	Polonaise	-do-	
MARTINEZ(Mannel)	29/9/1910 à Madrid(Espagne)	Espagnole	-do-	
JASTEK(Albert)	25/5/1891 à Prsognia(Polo-gne)	Polonaise	-do-	
NOWAK(Théophile)	14/4/1899 à Sandonis(-do-)	-do-	-do-	
NUNEZ(Emilio)	29/12/1916 à Bilbao(Espa-gne)	Espagnole	-do-	
PEREZ(Antonio)	18/4/1885 à Villa-Mayor(Espagne)	-do-	-do-	
PEIRERA(Abel)	15/2/1907 à Sédielos(Por-tugal)	Portugaise	-do-	
PONCELET(Nestor Joseph Charles)	10/4/1895 à Esnaux(Belgiqu)	Belge	-do-	
PONCELET,née Muller (Malbertine)	8/12/1895 à Lézi-Seraing (Belgique)	-do-	-do-	
PONCELET(Odile)	9/9/1919 à Seraing(Belgiqu)	Polonaise	-do-	
PAWLOWSKY(Agnès)	26/3/1904 à Lobez(Pologne)	-do-	-do-	
PANKER(Zalman)(J.)	2/5/1910 à Kalitz(-do-	-do-	-do-	
PANKER,née Tencer(J.)	28/5/1906 à Kalitz(-do-	-do-	-do-	
ROTA(Bono)	4/12/1899 à Poscante(Itali)	Italienne	-do-	
SELES(Antonio)	12/12/1894 à Riumes(-do-)	-do-	-do-	
SELES,née Brozowitch (Anna)	13/10/1894 à Augulin(Espa-gne)	Espagnole	-do-	
SUAREZ(Isaïs)	4/11/1914 à Mières(Espagne)	do	do	
TENCER(Brana)	4/7/1906 à Kalits(Pologne)	Polonaise	-do-	
ZAMPIERI(Angelo Augus-tin	28/4/1892 à San Guistino) (Italie)	Italienne	-do-	
ZAMPIERI,née Maérar (Elisabéth)	5/9/1899 à -do-	-do-	-do-	
ZAMPIERI( )	18.8.1912 à Pankow (Lézi-Seraing)	do	-do-	

Nom et prénoms	Date et lieu denaissance	Nationalite	Commune de résidence	ti
BINZTAK(Szcindga),J.)	2/10/1910 à Pidrkow(Polo	Polonaise	Dugeat	
FELDSTEIN(Nosa)(J.)	1/6/1918 à Lupzig(Pologne:	-do-	-do-	
HOCH,née Karmiol(Karole)(J.)	15/2/1896 à Stopnica(édo-:	-do-	-do-	
JANNERET(Paul)	24/4/1881 à Genève(Suisse:	Suisse	-do-	
KOMBOL(Zupan,Pétro)	28/6/1910 à Lator(Yougos-:lave	Yougoslave	-do-	
KOMBOL(Joseph)	6/6/1907 à Yargow(-do-)	-do-	-do-	
ANDREO(Miguel)	12/4/1901 à Vebis-Bàànco (Espagne)	Espagnole	-do-	
UHLMANN,née Straus (Clara Jeanne)(J.)	17/5/1876 à Liège(Belgique	Belge	-do-	
GAEZKA(Albert)(J.)	14/4/1909 à Gola(Pologne):	Polènaise	-do-	
SETTON(Cohen Rachelle:	4/9/1902 à Constantinople:	Constantine	-do-	
ABASTADO(née Nahmias (Dora) J.	24/7/1904 à Salonique	grecque	-do-	
ABASTADO(Nahan) J.	3/3/1892 à -do-	grecque	-do-	
RAFFAY(Stephan)	17/7/1897 à Felsoiger(Tché:coslovaquae)	Tchécoslovaque	Bennefond:	
RAFFAY(Jean)	29/11/1927 à Châlons-S-Marne.	-do-	-do-	
KU KOWA,Catherine)	18/4/1905 à Uslak(Tchécos:	-do-	-do-	
GIMENEZ-VERGARA(Antonio)	3/6/1904 à Tobarra(Espagne)	Espagnole	-do-	
WOJTOWIEZ(Julien)	16/2/1903 à Opatow(Pologn:Polonaise	Polonaise	Lestands	
MUSSO(Deminici)	28/4/1904 à Borgiallo(Ita:lie)	Italienne	-do-	
TEXEIRA(Antonio)	27/8/1902 à Amarante(Por-:tugal)	Portugaise	-do-	
TARABARIK(Jerko)	22/10/1913 à Mattos(You-:goslavie)	Yougoslave	-do-	
TOMACHEWSKI(André)	30/11/1899 à Asterade(Al-:lemagne)	Allemande	-do-	
GAVALI(Ottavio)	10/9/1912 à Valstagris (Italie)	Italienne	Murat	
ZANGA,Andréa;	26/10/1919 à Wall'Alto (Italie)	-do-	-do-	
BERNEJO(Serrano)	13/2/1917 à La Lema(Espa-:gne)	Espagnole	-do-	
MALYSZ,née Jakubina (Françoise)	16/9/1901 à Drzcieniec (Pologne)	Polonaise	Pradines	
BERNARDI,Barnabas,	16/12/1898 à Roccabruna (Italie)	Italienne	Pérols	
DA COSTA(Joaquin)	27/8/1904 à Sanjoan(Portu:gal)	Portugaise	-do-	
GONCALVES(Albano)	17/4/1910 à Conso(Pologne)	Italienne	-do-	
GONCALVES(Manuel)	29/8/1923 à Parmas-Guarda: (Portugal)	Portugaise	-do-	
GOLDNADEL(Mozjek) J.	25/11/1907 à Laskew(Polo-:gne)	Polonaise	-do-	
GONZALEZ,née Fernandez: Evangelina)	10/9/1911 à Avilès(Esp)	Espagnole	-do-	
HERRAIZ,née Martinez	20/11/1907 à Huertapelayo (Espagne)	Espagnole	-do-	
HERRAIZ,Florent,	3/1/1910 (-do-)	-do-	-do-	
FRYDMAN,Pysach) (J;)	20/10/1908 à Radon(Pologne	Polonaise	-do-	
LLOP,José,	17/1/1904 à Asco(Espagne)	Espagnole	-do-	
PEIRO,née Ribalta(Thérèse)	26/3/1912 à Barcelone(Esp:gne)	-do-	-do-	
ROZENT(Chaim) J.	26/5/1910 à Zirardow(Polo:Polonaise	Polonaise	-do-	

Nom et prénoms	Date et lieu de naissance	Nationalité	Commune de résidence	Observations
LANDMAN, Joahin Wolf. J.	25/3/1915 à Tarnow(Pologne)	Polonaise	Pérols	
HOZENT, née Krelmalka (Mika) J.	7/12/1916 à Lublin (-do-	-do-	-do-	
WOHL, Ruban) J.	14/10/1886 à Tarnapol -do-	-do-	-do-	
WEDNER, née Insel)J.	18/9/1907 à Halbuszowa-do-	-do-	-do-	
WEBNER (Israël) J.	28/11/1897 à Ubetszyki Dolme(Pologne)	-do-	-do-	dépôlem...
HALBZAJT, née Szejman (Chava) J.	15/5/1902 à Varsovie(Pologne)	-do-	-do-	
HALBZAJT(Abraham) J.	2/5/1904 à Varsovie(Polo-	-do-	-do-	
GRUN, née Jérousalins-ki(Rose) J.	3/2/1904 à Korelicht(-de-	-do-	-do-	
GRUN(Samuel) J.	3/5/1903 à Brzeske(Polo-)	-do-	-do-	Mariés
JEROUSALINSKI,née Sch-menwitz(Berthe) J.	10/2/1876à Kevelicht(Rus-sie)	Russe	-do-	
JEROUSALINSKI,Jacob)J	en juillet 1877 à Taurets (Russie)	-do-		
GUTWEIN,Osias, J.	en 1881 à Ozndec(Pologne)	Polonaise	-do-	
HOOTON (Edith)	2/1/1867 à Sydenham(Angl.	Anglaise	Tarnac	
MIRWIS,Tobias J.	13/2/1897 à Boxmeer(Holl.	Hollandaise	-do-	
ORLANDINI(Rosina)	8/1/1919 à Travestolo(It	Italienne	-do-	
PAWLAK(Andréa)	25/11/1906 à Krotoschin (Allemagne)	Allemande	-do-	
SZERDAVELYI,Ladislas J	26/10/1904 à Budapest(Hon	Hongroise	-do-	
GYJOWIEZ(Marie) J.	10/12/1924 à Diaslosyn(Po	Polonaise	-do-	
GYJOWIEZ(Bela) J.	9/8/1927 à (-do-)	-do-	-do-	
DEHAAFF,née Masters (Ray) J.	5/5/1903 à Londres(Angl.	Anglaise	-do-	
VAN-GELDEREN(Philippe)(J.)	8/3/1883 à Schiedam(Holl.	Hollandaise	-do-	
VAN-GELDEREN,née Cals-Stienze) J.	14/6/1885 à Gonda(Hollande	-do-	-do-	
SPIRA,née Mire Ryfka J	11/11/1880 à Rgessone(Polo	Polonaise	-do-	
MONHEIT,née Silberman (Rose) J.	12/10/1889 à Rudzewos(-do-	-do-	-do-	
DRESNER(Hena) J.	4/5/1904 à Nyfeheite(Rou	Roumaine	-do-	
DRESNER(Hensy) J.	5/2/1907 à Chust(Roumanie	-do-	-do-	
WAJWSZTOK(Fradja) J.	15/5/1880 à Naisielak(Pol	Polonaise	-do-	
BLUSZTEYN(Frymila)J.	5/5/1901 à Wyszogrod(-do-	-do-	-do-	
FRIEDMANN,Cécilia J.	20/8/1907 à Michalova(Tché coslovaquie)	Tchécoslaque	-do-	
BAJTWER,Bagla J.	25/6/1910 àZarmonvice(Pol	Polonaise	-do-	::
LEBOVITS,Guillaume J.	1/5/1897 à Feukste Ardo (Hongrie)	Hongroise	-do-	
WIZENBERG,Mager, J.	27/9/1904 Larsezow(Pol.	Polonaise	-do-	mariés
WIZENBERG,Maya) J/	25/10/1908 à Zamose(-do-)	-do-	-do-	
SCHEINHAUS(Léopold)J.	24/8/1886 à Radischkowits (Russie)	Russe	-do-	
MORAS(Antonio)	28/7/1898 à Casarès Mala-ga(Espagne)	Espagnole	Toy-Viam	
SARAMIENTO,Elvira)	2/2/1894	-do-	-do-	
MAYER,née Schloss J.	1/2/1885 à ....(Roumanie)	Roumaine	-do-	
KWIBEL(Bernard) J.	26/6/1887 à Bucarest(Rou-manie)	Roumaine	-do-	
KLEEBLATT,Renée J.	13/4/1911 à Dusemond(Luxem bourg.	Belgique	-do-	
GHETZER,Wolf) J.	1/6/1898 à Urecévie(Pol.	Polonaise	-do-	
JACOBI, Jekheskiel)J.	2/11/1897 à Naschelsk(Rus	Russe	-do-	
JACOBI(Régina) J.	18/12/1902 à Krementschok (Russie)	-do-	-do-	

Nom et prénoms	Date et lieu de naissance	Nationalité	Commune de résidence	Obse tic
BERCOVICI(Malvina) J?	:5/5/1907 à Sighet(Hongrie)	:Hongroise	Toy-Viam	
OLSZYCKA(Srul) J.	:en 1880 à Sudlie(Pologne	:Polonaise	-do-	
FORUNY(Salvador)	:23/7/1922 à Terragona(Esp	:Espagnole	:St.Merd.	
FORTUNY(Joaquin)	:7/8/1924 à -do- -do-	:-do-	-do-	
FORTUNY(Ascensio)	:13/1/1895 à Dlever(Espagne)	:-do-	-do-	
MARTIN(Félisa)	:21/2/1910 à Santander(Esp:	:-do-	-do-	
MARTINEZ(Pédro)	:3/1/1913 à Huertapelayo (Espagne)	:-do-	-do-	
MARTINEZ(Dionisio)	:9/4/1916 à -do-	:-do-	-do-	
MARTINEZ(Isabelle)	:2/7/1887 à -do-	:-do-	-do-	
MARTINEZ(Pédro)	:23/10/1860 à -do-	:-do-	-do-	
ADONDI(Eugène)	:11/3/1915 à Unchio Intro (Italie)	:Italienne	Viam	
BEKZADIAN(Paul)	:16/10/1901 à Erzeroun(Arménia)	:Arménienne	-do-	
BEKZADIAN(Olga)	:8/6/1902 à Tiplis(Caucase	:Russe	-do-	
CORNELIO(Henriette)	:8/4/1896 à Valence(Espagne	:Espagnole	-do-	
CORNELIO(Floréal)	:25/1/1928 à Port de Bouc (B.d.Rh)	:-do-	-do-	
DOS REIS(Francisco)	:16/9/1900 à Troncose(Portugal)	:Portugaise	-do-	
IGLESIAS(Ruffino)	:23/8/1911 à Madrid(Espagne	:Espagnole	-do-	
KELECEMIC(Dimitri)	:10/12/1907 à Diva(Yougosl	:Yougoslave	-do-	
MORENO, née Martinez (Victoria)	:1/11/1907 à Carthagène (Espagne)	:Espagnole	-do-	
MORENO(José)	:18/4/1909 à Velez-Blance (Espagne)	:-do-	-do-	
PALLAS(Georges)	:23/4/1863 à Ortilla(Esp)	:-do-	-do-	
VENTURA, née Sallès (Rosa)	:5/8/1907 à Castellan -do-:	:-do-	-do-	

A Bugeat, le 10 Août 1943

Le Gendarme JOURGETOUX, Commandant provisoirement la brigade

vu et transmis
utsel le 14 Août 1943
le Lieutenant ...

PRÉFECTURE
DE LA CORRÈZE

Cabinet du Préfet
JR/JM
Référence n° 3486

18 Avril 1944

TULLE, le

Le Préfet de la Corrèze
à Monsieur le Chef du Gouvernement
Ministre, Secrétaire d'État à l'Intérieur
Service des Relations Franco-allemandes

à Monsieur le Chef du Gouvernement
Ministre, Secrétaire d'État à l'Intérieur
Direction des Services d'Administration

V I C H Y

à Monsieur le Préfet Régional
- Cabinet -

L I M O G E S

ADMISSE
-1 MAI 1944

OBJET. - arrestations opérées par les autorités allemandes.

Le 6 avril 1944, des militaires appartenant aux troupes d'
opérations, ont procédé à l'arrestation de 16 personnes, dont 5
enfants, dans la commune de BUGEAT.

Ce sont les nommés :

1°) - KLEINBERG Marie, née IZBICKA, née le 26/5/1903, nationalité polonaise, race juive.

2°) - HOCH, née KERLINOL Karola, née le 13/2/1885, nationalité
polonaise, race juive.

3°) - UHLMANN née KLARA Jeanne, le 13/3/1876, nationalité belge
race juive.

4°) - FRIBOURG née HACH Lucie, née le 17/7/1873, nationalité
française, race juive.

5°) - ROSANT Chaïm, né le 26/5/1910, manoeuvre, nationalité
polonaise, race juive.

6°) - TANCER Brana, née le 4/7/1906, nationalité polonaise,
race juive.

Les 2 enfants de Mme KLEINBERG, âgés respectivement de 11 et
ans, ses deux nièces de 15 et 5 ans qui vivaient avec elle ont
été emmenés ainsi que le fils de Mme TANCER, âgé de 4 ans.

D'autre part, ces militaires se sont faits conduire par M.
le Président de la Délégation Spéciale de BUGEAT au hameau de l'
Echameil, Cne de BUGEAT. Ils ont perquisitionné dans la maison des
époux VACHER, et après avoir fait sortir les propriétaires, ils
ont incendié leur maison et les ont arrêtés.

Par la suite, dans ce même hameau, ils ont découvert un tract

LETTER FROM THE PREFECT OF CORRÈZE
TO THE HEAD OF THE VICHY GOVERNMENT,
18 APRIL 1944

Report dated 18 April 1944
From the Prefect of Corrèze, Tulle

Copies addressed to the Secretaries of State dealing
with Franco-German relations and Armistice
Administration in the Vichy Government,
and to the Regional Prefect in Limoges.

Re: arrests carried out by German authorities

On 6 April 1944, military personnel of the operational forces
carried out the arrest of 16 persons, including 5 children, in the
commune of Bugeat.

These are as follows:

1) KLEINBERG Marie, née IZBICKA, born 26.5.1903,
   nationality Polish, race Jew
2) HOCH, née KERKINOL Karola, born 15.2.1885, nationality Polish, race Jew
3) UHLMANN née KLARA Jeanne, 15.5.1876, nationality
   Belgian, race Jew
4) FRIBOURG née HACH Lucie, born 17.7.1873, nationality
   French, race Jew
5) ROSENT Chaim, born 26.5.1910, manual worker, nationality Polish, race Jew
6) TENCER Brana, born 4.7.1906, nationality Polish, race Jew

The two children of Mme Kleinberg, respectively 11 and 9 years
old and her two nieces, aged 15 and 5, who were living with her
were also taken, as was the son of Mme Tencer, aged 4.

vraisemblablement collé par des réfractaires.

Pour ce motif, ils ont arrêté tous les hommes du hameau, soit
M. GOURINAL, GANNE et NAUCHE.

A 11, h 30, trois gendarmes de la brigade de EUGEAT, circulant
dans la région ont croisé les soldats allemands qui discutaient avec
ces 4 hommes.

Quelques instants après, ils ont entendu plusieurs rafales
de mitraillettes.

A leur retour, ces gendarmes ont aperçu, au même endroit, les
cadavres des 4 hommes, criblés de balles.

M. le Président de la Délégation Spéciale de EUGEAT a été
immédiatement avisé de ces faits.

La destination prise par les personnes arrêtées est inconnue.

Le Préfet,

JMD/JP Copie transmise pour information à Monsieur l'Intendant du
Maintien de l'Ordre.

A LIMOGES, le

LE PREFET REGIONAL,

In addition, the same troops were accompanied by the President of the Special Delegation in Bugeat to the hamlet of L'Echameil in the Commune of Bugeat. They searched the premises of the Vacher husband and wife, and after having obliged the owners to leave the house, they set fire to it and arrested the couple.

Subsequently, in the same hamlet, they discovered a tract that had probably been posted by recalcitrants.

On these grounds they arrested all the men of the hamlet, namely

M. GOURINAL, M. GANNE and M. NAUCHE

At 11.30 a.m., three gendarmes from the Bugeat brigade, patrolling in the vicinity, passed a group of German soldiers in discussion with these four men.

Shortly thereafter, they heard several volleys of machine gun fire.

On their return from patrol, the gendarmes discovered, at that precise location, the bodies of the four men, riddled with bullets.

The President of the Special Delegation in Bugeat was immediately informed of these facts.

The destination of the persons who were arrested is unknown.

SIGNED
THE PREFECT

Copy forwarded for information to the Intendant for the Maintenance of Law and Order by the Regional Prefect, Limoges.